SHACKLED
TO MY
FAMILY

SAMINA YOUNIS

Oxford eBooks

Contents

Introduction

MY NAME IS Samina. I was born along with an identical twin sister to very strict Pakistani-born parents. As Muslims, they prayed 5 times each day without fail, and like many of their generation had an arranged marriage.

My sister and I were regarded as a burden by my parents; as girls, the family name could not be carried on through us. Ultimately my parents believed that one day we would bring shame upon them. They were determined to have male offspring to carry on the family name and so the family grew quite large in their attempt to raise boys.

My story is a first-hand account of how I was raised in a strict Pakistani Muslim family and knowing that from an early age my life was already planned out for me. I was constantly reminded by my parents that a woman's place is in the home, that women do not have a voice in society and must only speak when spoken to.

From childhood through to my teenage years, I became emotionally and mentally scarred by the violence and abuse I experienced from my parents. I grew to learn that the honour of my family was more important to my parents than the lives of my sisters and I.

My mother would watch my every move in the hope of provoking my father to beat me. He was even stricter than my mother and he would beat me with anything that was to hand at the time.

As I grew older I longed for the freedom of Western culture, such as wearing lipstick and eye-liner but my parents were immensely disapproving of such things. My parents' views on Western culture were very bizarre; my father thought Western women were prostitutes and sinners while my mother believed that using tampons would 'ruin my virginity' and I would no longer be pure. This made my parents more determined to stop Western influences from entering our home and minds to preserve the family's honour.

Watching television was almost banned in the home but exceptions were made if there was something my father wanted to watch, though we would try to catch the occasional programme when my parents were not at home.

My parents' harassment caused me to become detached from day-to-day life. School became very difficult and the thought of going home afterwards sent tears rolling down my cheeks. I found myself talking to God on a regular basis, asking him to take my life or to make my parents kinder. I felt that God was not listening to me, he disliked me and to punish me he sent unkind people to be my parents.

I knew that a forced marriage was my destiny as I had seen my elder sisters suffer the same fate.

Later, the sudden death of my father became a turning point in my truly miserable existence.

1 First Memories

IT WAS THE winter of 1990 and I was six years old. Preparations were under way for my first trip to Pakistan; I would be travelling there with my sister Shazia and this was the very first time I had been away from home, so you can imagine my excitement.

I had only just had my passport photograph taken, everything was done in such a hurry. But my excitement soon changed when I saw my twin sister Aisha and learned that she was not going with me. We had never been apart before, it felt like she was the other half of me and I was leaving her behind. I recall her face, so drawn as she asked me if I wanted her colouring book to take with me.

The following morning, my father took Shazia and I to the airport. I remember him buying me a packet of crisps - cheese and onion flavour. I was in tears, he kissed me on the cheek and left. At that point I was no longer interested in going to Pakistan I just wanted to go home.

On the aeroplane, the air hostess gave me a children's goody bag which contained a small packet of pencil crayons, a colouring book and a pack of playing cards. This soon took my mind off things.

The whole purpose of this trip was to obtain a visa for Shazia's husband. She was married a few years earlier to my uncle's son, Kabir.

Shazia and I were very close - she had been more like a

mother to me since my early childhood. My mother had my brother Abdul to take care of and Aisha was looked after by my second elder sister Fatima.

I remember sharing a bed with Shazia and she used to read to me at bed time. Shazia's English was not very good but she tried her best.

My father came to England from Pakistan a lot earlier than my mother in search of a better life and seven years later, my mother came across with my three oldest sisters.

Pakistan was always the hot topic in my family. I remember seeing blue envelopes with 'Air Mail' written on them. Everyone used to get really excited when one would arrive. The letters were always from my elder uncle Farooq on my father's side. He was very well educated and had fought in the Pakistani Army. He had always dreamt of coming to England and visiting London.

I remember feeling the cold of winter as we arrived in Islamabad; we were greeted by my uncle Farooq at the airport. I also remember seeing lots of homeless and poor people, most of which had severe disfigurements. My uncle Farooq told them to go away and my sister and I were told not to give them money - he said they are not worth pitying.

The journey from Islamabad to Azad Kashmir, which literally means 'free Kashmir', was very long and bumpy. There were a lot of potholes as we approached the villages and the roads quickly gave way to simple dirt tracks. Along the way we passed cows, sheep and goats roaming about without a care in the world. We were going to stay with the extended family in a village outside of the Mirpur district.

As a child visiting Pakistan and being British born I was treated like royalty. News of our arrival in Pakistan spread quickly and people came from all over the village just to say hello.

While I was there I had to dress according to the custom

which meant wearing the traditional salwar kameez and a scarf. I remember being made a fuss of and being teased for not knowing how to speak Urdu and the Kashmiri language.

While I was in Pakistan I went to a local school where I learned a little Urdu and I also witnessed a goat being slaughtered. This was the first time I really understood what halal (lawful) meat was.

I was also invited to a wedding; it was amazing! I was allowed to dress up in a colourful salwar kameez and eat lots of delicious food. I also learned how to clean using a brush made entirely from straw. I even learned how to milk cows and to use cow manure for a fire.

A couple of months passed there and we were back home. My experiences and memories of my first time in Pakistan were wonderful.

Soon after, my brother-in-law's visa came through and he came to England. After that, I was no longer Shazia's first priority and I had to move out of her room and into my parents' room.

The room consisted of a double bed in the centre in which my mother and brother Abdul slept. There was another bed on the other side of the room in which my father slept and a sofa bed in which I had to sleep.

For nights on end I used to cry myself to sleep because I missed Shazia so much. I used to wait up for her in the mornings before she went to work and wave at her through the window. I was caught by my father a few times and beaten for waking up.

Shackled to my Family

2 Fear

MY FATHER WAS the head of the house. He was a very tall, strong man with a long, grey beard and large, piercing eyes. He was a traditional Muslim Pakistani man who wore a salwar kameez and prayed five times a day. He had previously travelled to Mecca in Saudi Arabia and fulfilled the fifth pillar of Islam called *Hajj*.

In the Pakistani community he was known as *Hajji* - a very respectful name. He also taught young children how to read the Holy Quran.

My father was a lot older than my mother; she was in fact half his age and had always been a housewife, looking after the house and children but never herself. She always covered her head with a head-scarf and wore a salwar kameez. They were forced into an arranged marriage at an early age when my mother was just fifteen. As far as I remember she had no friends or social life - looking after the family was all she knew.

My father spent most of his time either at the mosque or watching television - anything about Pakistan, the news, wildlife or cricket but Pakistan had to be playing cricket. He never helped my mother with any of the household chores or with the children. He did not believe he should help around the house and always thought it was a women's duty and this duty fell upon my mother as his wife.

My early education was at a school which my father had

chosen because my third eldest sister, Yasmin used to go there. I loved my primary school years, I loved learning. Being at school gave me a sense of peace, somewhere where I could be myself but each day that peace was broken when I had to return home.

Home life went from bad to worse. My mother continuously cursed Aisha and I because she wanted us to have been born boys. My brother Abdul was born with a cleft lip and palate which WE were blamed for. We were used as punch bags during my parents' frequent arguments and constantly told that we should have died at birth. I remember feeling isolated and wanted to run away but I was always told never to tell any of our teachers or friends about what went on at home. If we did, they said, people would come and take us away and do horrible things to us.

Abdul was never blamed for anything; he would get us into trouble and it was never his fault, we would be punished. My father would drag us kicking and screaming into the darkest and scariest part of the house, the middle room of the cellar. There were no windows there and he would tie us up and lock us in the dark after we had been beaten with his rubber slipper or favourite stick. I remember feeling really scared, not knowing what else was down in the cellar, in the dark with us. He would leave us there for hours and make ghost-like noises and scare us by pulling at our legs. Our hearts would be pounding and we struggled to catch our breath. My mother never came to help us, no one ever did.

Punishment from my father was administered on a daily basis, he would beat me for no reason. Even if he called my name, he would throw his slipper at me first to get my attention. I sometimes hid my father's slipper in the hope of him not finding it. He would spend time looking for it, and the more time he spent searching, the happier I was because he would forget about beating me when he eventually found his slipper.

Making friends at school was never easy as I had no confidence. I was always scared of speaking or asking a question. My mother always said to us "Never question anything" so we never did. We were never helped with our homework; as far as my parents were concerned going to school was not down to them, it was forced upon them by the government. Abdul's education was more important because he was a boy, the superior race in my parents' eyes. Abdul was the one who would carry on the family name. Aisha and I were always told we would not be going to college or university. We were not allowed to speak English at home because English was considered to be our second language and Urdu was the first. My mother could not speak English, she never learned how to and my father's English just about got him by.

Aisha and I were never allowed to have Western or English friends at school and certainly no male friends. My mother called them "the devil's children" so we had to stay away. Her fear was that we would be influenced by different cultures and lead astray. I remember feeling really nervous talking to a male teacher because I always thought men were frightening and intimidating. Our parents constantly reminded us by saying "We are Muslims, we do not do anything that would be seen as unlawful or something that would damage or destroy the family's dignity and reputation." This was very hard for us as all we really wanted to do was to interact with other children and do what other children did.

Every day after school we were forced to read the Holy Quran, even Abdul was not exempt from this. My father said that teaching the Holy Quran was one of his duties as a Muslim father. Aisha and I had to cover our heads with a scarf and wash ourselves properly before we started reciting verses. We were not allowed to leave until we had learned every last word and read it back twice word-perfect. If we didn't, we were hit with a stick or slapped in the face. At times we were in tears because we were in so much pain. My father showed us no mercy, he always thought punishment and fear were the key to making us remember what he taught us.

On one occasion my third eldest sister Yasmin who was at secondary school at the time brought some pop magazines home. They had pictures and posters of boy bands. She stuck one poster of a well-known pop singer on her bedroom wall. My father beat her so much that her arms were bruised, her back was bleeding, her glasses had cut her nose and had broken. He ripped everything up and threw it all in the bin.

As children, we were never allowed pocket money to buy sweets. My mother and father would say "Children who get pocket money are spoilt and freedom is frowned upon."

The only time we ever did get any money was on Eid day and that was only 50p. Eid day was a day of celebration for a Muslim and for me this seemed to be the only time when my parents were kind and the physical and mental abuse would stop. It felt like my parents were on holiday from their full time jobs. We would always look forward to our father coming home from the mosque on Eid day so we could have our present of 50p. Straight away we would run to the corner shop and buy sweets or chocolate. Eid in our family when we were growing up was always something we looked forward to because this was one of the occasions when we were allowed to get dressed up in fancy Pakistani clothes; the only other occasions were weddings.

On Eid day mother would always wake us up with warm sawaiyan - noodles in milk and sugar. After we had eaten we would get changed into our fancy clothes which my mother had sewn, or the clothes were sent from Pakistan by our close relatives. Meanwhile, my father went to the mosque to carry out the Eid prayer. We would wait for him to come home and then we would get our present from him. After that we would eat our Eid meal which was always brown rice with lamb or chicken. My parents were always at their happiest when it was

Eid; Ramadan was over and they felt at ease because they had completed one of the most important pillars of Islam.

My father would always tell us stories of Islam and the prophets of Allah. He was very spiritual and always said "This life is nothing compared to the thereafter." It was very rare to see my father give affection or show any emotion but when it came to Islam and religion he would become very emotional, it was as though he was a different person. Islam meant everything to him.

Shackled to my Family

3 A boy is born

A COUPLE OF years later, my younger brother Hamid was born. I remember my mother and father being overwhelmed with joy, they were so thankful to Allah to finally have another son.

A year later, we moved into a bigger house because there were now eleven people living together. My mother, father, elder sister Shazia and her husband Kabir, my second elder sister Fatima, my third elder sister Yasmin, myself, Aisha and my two brothers Abdul and Hamid.

This house was a 4 bedroom semi-detached. The attic was where Shazia and her husband slept and the second bedroom was where Fatima and Aisha slept. The third bedroom was my parents' room where my two brothers Abdul and Hamid slept. The smallest bedroom was for Yasmin and I.

I was made to move out of my parents' room when Hamid was born. My parents did not want Yasmin to have a room all to herself as that meant she would have a degree of freedom.

A couple of years later, my father helped Shazia buy her first home. It was a terraced house with three bedrooms. My father had organised students to rent the house for a year or two and he kept all of the extra income that came in. Shazia worked very hard in a factory sewing clothes to pay for her mortgage and she also supported her husband Kabir. This was her first home and soon she had to move out when she was expecting her first child - a boy! Everyone was really happy except my mother;

there was a distinct sense of jealousy from her towards Shazia because she had to have five girls before she had a boy.

Shazia always felt that my mother did not love her as much as she wanted her to, she simply would not show any feelings towards her. When Wasim, my first nephew was born, my father was overwhelmed with happiness; he brought boxes of mithai (fresh Indian sweets) to celebrate. I remember seeing the fridge overloaded with mithai which was distributed amongst family and friends.

I was told that mithai was given to express the joy and happiness of having another boy born into the family; it was also traditionally given out during weddings.

My brother-in-law Kabir never helped Shazia look after Wasim; he was incredibly lazy and did not really want to do anything. She did everything herself; she paid the bills and worked as a full time housewife. Kabir could not speak English and refused to learn the language. As he was uneducated he found it very difficult to get a job of any sort. To help Shazia out, my mother and father used to send me to her house to help her do the cleaning and to look after Wasim. I didn't mind because I got to spend time with Shazia who I missed dearly.

During this time, I learned a lot about Shazia and Kabir's relationship. He was not the loving husband I first thought he was. He rushed Shazia into making him a resident of this country and once that had happened he changed, knowing that now no matter what happened in their relationship he would never be deported.

His family in Pakistan would constantly write or call to speed up the process. She was always tearful when she spoke to my mother about it and said she wished things were different. Shazia had a forced marriage which had been decided from the moment she was born. My father was never prepared to listen to any argument against it; it was his brother, Ahmed's son she was to marry.

There were always arguments about money in their home. Kabir's family would write letters asking for money to be sent. Shazia had just bought a house, she saved very hard for years to buy it and Kabir without a job was claiming job-seekers allowance from the government.

After Wasim was born, Shazia became a full-time mother with no income except for child benefit. She was really struggling and yet Kabir's family were constantly pressurising Shazia to send them money. She used to say to Kabir "We have no money to support our own family, how can we send money that we don't have to yours?" Then the arguments would start again and he would say "The house in Pakistan needs repairing" or "Father has no income" but his father had a hardware store in the village which was always busy.

Returning home after spending weeks at Shazia's house was always really hard. I used to hate it and I begged Shazia, with tears in my eyes to let me stay.

Sharing a bedroom with Yasmin was fun. She was at secondary school at the time and would tell me stories about what she did every day and what it was like being with friends and having laughter brighten her day. She told me that she could be herself around her friends.

Yasmin found it very difficult to study at home because she was forced to carry out household duties such as cooking and cleaning. By the time she had finished doing the chores it was too late to start her homework and she had do her very best at school the following day. Yasmin knew my father's views on higher education, she knew she would not be allowed to attend college and so it did not matter if she had the top grades.

Yasmin failed most of her GCSEs as soon as she turned sixteen then left school. She had no option but to listen to my father and concede to his wishes. She was told she would only be allowed to attend college if she married.

Shackled to my Family

4 Forced to marry

YASMIN WAS VERY unhappy about the forced marriage, but she agreed to go ahead with it. She was promised to be married to my uncle Iqbal's son, my mother's nephew in Pakistan. Yasmin had never met her husband-to-be; all she knew was that his name was Arshad and he was four years older than her. My mother made this decision because my father had chosen who Shazia was to marry and she thought it only fair to include her family in the marriages.

Fatima, my second eldest unmarried sister was to be married at the same time. She was promised to my Uncle Farooq's son, Kamran.

Fatima and Yasmin were to be married in Pakistan in the coming summer. Fatima was four years older than Yasmin and I always thought she was more like my parents. She was always thought of as the 'clever one' in my parents' eyes because she never rebelled against anything and always sought my parents' love and attention. She never got on with Shazia.

Fatima convinced Shazia into thinking that she was hated by my parents and that she was really never part of the family in the first place. This was very hurtful as Shazia would never do anything to hurt anyone; she was always so quiet and gentle.

I was nine years old at the time of the weddings and I remember seeing lots and lots of nice things that were being bought for the occasion. I really wanted to go to Pakistan for the weddings but I was not allowed because I had been before a few years earlier. I loved going to weddings and dressing up but this time it was Aisha's turn to experience Pakistan.

Aisha had never been to Pakistan before. She was so excited and I was so jealous. My family used to say "Pakistan is where the heart is" and "Eventually this is where all of us will be buried."

My father was going to Pakistan with Fatima, Yasmin, Aisha and my brother Abdul. My mother was not going because she was looking after my younger brother Hamid and I. Also, my father felt it was his duty to be one to give his daughters away.

I remember feeling really sad because I wanted to go to Pakistan but I was told I would go when I am older. At the time I thought nothing of it.

The day came when they were leaving. I remember seeing five large suitcases, all of them were filled to the brim with clothes. A lot of the suitcases contained gifts for the extended family; they used to say "Things are very expensive in Pakistan." I later found out this was not true, they just did not want to spend their own money and wanted everything for free. They thought my family were well off.

Once they had gone to Pakistan, things were very quiet. I no longer had anyone to talk to, my mother was always busy with household duties and all I could do was to go to the park and play on the swings for a while. Afterwards, I often went to the local play centre where I got to meet different children without my mother knowing. Other times, I would simply go to my room, although I would often get told off for being in my room for too long; my mother hated it. During this time my father would try to call at least once a week.

On the week of the weddings we had a call from my father saying both of the weddings were going to go ahead on the same day. The reason for this was that the groom's family were not willing to pay for the wedding receptions. The wedding preparations along with the ceremonies took roughly a week. The sad thing was that my sisters were unable to attend each other's weddings and the family was split up.

Once the weddings were over, everyone came back home. Aisha told me she had a wonderful time as I did when I went. She had no idea that while she was over there she had been promised to my maternal cousin.

I was able to see video footage of both of the weddings. I remember thinking they were not as magical as I thought they would have been. There were hundreds of people there; most of them were from big families ranging from four to nine children per household. I later found out that those families were only interested in seeing how wealthy our family was and if there were any possible wedding proposals to be made.

My sisters looked really unhappy. Both Yasmin and Fatima had their heads lowered and just looked at the floor. I asked my mother why they looked so unhappy, my mother's answer was "They are not supposed to look happy, they are getting married."

On the day of the wedding I remember seeing my father cry as my sisters were leaving the family home and going to their husband's home. It was a complete shock seeing him like that as he had always looked angry and never showed any emotion.

The holiday season was over and my sisters were married. My parents had a weight lifted off their shoulders. My father used to say "Now they are married they are no longer our concern."

5   Father's control

FATIMA SUCCESSFULLY GOT herself a job as a nursery nurse and started saving up for a house with the intention of calling her husband over from Pakistan - well at least this was what my parents thought. All of Fatima's earnings went into my father's bank account; she was still very much controlled by him even though she was married. He used to say "I am doing this for your own good so you do not spend all of your money and so you can learn the value of money." She used to beg him for even something as little as £5 and he would always ask her why she wanted it.

I was still sharing a room with Yasmin, and she would tell me stories about college life and what it was like. She was very different from Shazia or Fatima. She was re-taking her GCSEs and was doing really well, She said to me that she wanted to work hard and prove to my father that she was clever, that she could get good results and be someone. But he always told her that she would never amount to anything and continue to beat her up.

Yasmin felt trapped. She did not love her husband, Arshad and said to me that she was forced into the marriage that was arranged from the moment she was born.

My parents knew how she felt about him but chose to ignore it as the two families were united and if she did divorce, the family's reputation would be in tatters. Arshad wrote love letters to Yasmin but she was forced to respond back to them through our father.

Studying helped Yasmin as she felt that she could escape to somewhere better and it helped her take her mind off things. She also wanted to prove to my father that she was worth something. Sometimes she stayed late after college hours for extra tuition but my father would always end up beating her. My mother was adding fuel to the fire by saying to my father "she is not where she was saying she was" implying that she had a boyfriend, and this was forbidden.

Yasmin was rebelling against everything, she just wanted to be heard. Most nights, Yasmin used to cry herself to sleep after father had hit her for wanting to do something that he did not agree with. She felt there was nothing she could do. She used to try to stand up for herself and say "all I want is an education" or "can I please have Miriam around tonight, we are discussing a monologue for English?" but my father and mother both hated that and again she was punished.

I remember thinking she had courage to ask in the first place even though she knew she would not get what she wanted. She wished she could go out with her friends from college in the evenings or even to their house but she was afraid to ask; she knew what the answer would be.

Our parents did not care how they treated us. If we had visitors at the house, our parents would still beat us in front of them. Yasmin's friend's parents were not as strict as ours. Even though most of Yasmin's friends were Pakistani they were allowed to wear at least some western clothing.

Yasmin would buy make-up with her pocket money which she saved for weeks on end and would wear it just before she left the house as she caught the bus to college, she would also untie her hair and let it down. Before she came home she would take all of her make-up off and tie her hair back up again.

The pocket money which she got from my father was not

very much at all, just £3.00 a week. This money had to pay for her lunch at college. My parents hated young girls - especially those who were not married or wearing make-up because they were seen as tempting the opposite sex. My mother never wore make-up, not even on her wedding day.

Most of the time, Yasmin was searched before she left the house because my mother was always suspicious of her. One occasion when my mother searched Yasmin, she caught her with a lipstick in her bag and she was beaten once more and the lipstick taken away from her and destroyed.

A couple of years passed and my mother had another baby - a girl. I remember thinking we had a big enough family already but my parents were trying for another boy. But they were disappointed again; they saw the child, the sixth girl in the family now, as another burden. My sister Laila was born much darker than the rest of us; my father called her the "black sheep of the family."

Growing up, Laila was teased for her colour by my parents, brothers and sisters and the kids at school; she was pushed about like a rag-doll.

During this time my brothers-in-law were writing constantly to my parents wanting to know why my sisters had not filed for their visas. Fatima and Yasmin did not want anything to do with them, there was no emotional connection or love between the two couples. I also felt that Fatima was copying Yasmin's decisions and felt she had to because Yasmin seemed a lot more confident in what she wanted in life.

My parents were very ashamed and at breaking point. They felt there was nothing else they could do apart from beating Fatima and Yasmin. They hoped that using violence might shock them into listening and thought that was the right thing to do.

A year or two had passed and still my sisters refused to call their husbands over to England. They had no contact with them despite their letters and phone calls. My parents had to lie saying they were both busy with their education.

6 Father's death

MY MOTHER HAD her ninth child. She was still hoping for another boy but it was a girl again - her name was Nadia. Before my mother fell pregnant she was told by the doctors not to have any more children as her health was seriously at risk. During my mother's last pregnancy she was told that there was a very high risk the child might be severally disabled but my parents ignored the doctor's advice and went ahead with the pregnancy in the hope of the child being born a boy. Nadia was the last child that my parents had. She grew especially attached to my father as my mother had to take care of the other children.

Aisha and I had finished primary school and were now going to a girls only secondary school which was chosen by my father. Again this was the same school that Fatima and Yasmin went to and the same school which most of the other Pakistani parents in our area sent their daughters to.

Going to this school was really tough for me as I felt we were following in Fatima's and Yasmin's footsteps.

Although the school had a large number of Pakistani pupils, the school's reputation or background did not matter to my father. All that mattered was that it was a girls only school and boys were not allowed. Making friends from outside the Pakistani community was really hard because we were not allowed to have any other friends. But gradually at school it became easier to interact with different ethnicities during our lessons.

My father was still very much in control. He used to drop us off at school and then in the afternoon would return to wait for us at the school gates.

My brother Abdul had started secondary school, he was a year younger than us. He was very quiet in public but he looked up to my father and he loved the fact that boys were supposedly the superior race. He used to create arguments and enjoyed it when my father or mother would punish us for something which we did not do. I used to think that he would turn out just like my father.

My mother and father could see that we were starting to become young teenagers. I remember the time I had my first period, I was too scared to tell anyone. I really did not know what to do but thankfully, my teacher at school reassured me and told me all about it. I was so afraid of telling my mother, I thought I had done something wrong so I told Fatima instead and she told my mother who in turn told my father. He slapped me across the head and my mother just cursed me. I was made to feel that it was something to be ashamed of and not something natural.

My mother and Fatima both told me never to use a tampon as it would 'ruin' my virginity and it would bring shame upon them. After that I felt my parents always kept an extra eye on me.

Two years had passed since we started secondary school and nothing had changed. At home things were going from bad to worse. My mother was arguing more and more with my father because she was left to care for the children and she always felt that he never pulled his weight. I was constantly scared of coming home from school just in case I was beaten up for no reason.

It was April 1997. My father did not take Aisha and I to school that particular morning and we had to catch the bus for the very first time. The car was not working and had been at the garage being repaired for most of the day. We came home from school as per usual and we did not read the Holy Quran, my father was not there to teach us and I did not see him at all that evening.

I was woken up by cries from Fatima and our mother. My father had just finished his evening prayer and had collapsed on the floor, unconscious. Yasmin and I rushed into the bedroom. We did not know what to do at first; I thought my father was pretending as he did from time to time. But he wasn't. Fatima had his head in her lap and was trying to wake him. The ambulance was called and my father's sister who we did not really get along with was also called. When the ambulance arrived, my father was taken to the hospital along with his sister.

We heard no news until the morning, when it was announced that my father had suffered a heart attack and had died. An autopsy was carried out on my father's body which in Islam is not allowed but we were told it had to be done due to his sudden death.

The following day we were surrounded by relatives and friends of the family who wanted to pay their respects. My father was very well thought of in the Pakistani community. There were people at the funeral that I had never seen before, people who when my father was alive we did not get on with.

I remember thinking this was all a dream. I thought my father would live forever because he always had such a hold and impact on us. I also felt a sense of relief at his passing as I felt the most terrifying person who I had known was gone and I was no longer afraid.

Straight after the funeral, my father's body was flown to Pakistan. My mother went with the body along with Fatima,

Hamid and my younger sister Nadia who was only four at the time.

For weeks after the funeral we were visited by cousins. We had not been in contact with one of them as she had been forced into marriage to my uncle Farooq's son - she wanted a divorce. My cousins became really close to us now that my father had gone; there was no one standing in the way any more.

For months felt as though my father was still with us. I used to wake up thinking everything had been a dream. I would imagine that I had seen him crossing the street or hear him shout my name.

Months passed and my mother was back at home. She was never the same, she did not have my father to fall back on and was lost without him. She felt like she was pushed into the deep end. Before, she was completely oblivious to what my father did, she did not know how to pay the bills or do the simplest tasks like going to the supermarket and doing the weekly grocery shopping. She became so distant.

I remember thinking she thought we were to blame. She said on one occasion that our birth had been the cause of great stress to him. The stress of what the girls would do as they grew older that might bring disgrace to the family. She used to say "You girls kept us awake at night."

7 Desperation

AISHA AND I went back to school; my mother had no trust in us. We had to justify everything we did - what we did at school, who our friends were. I used to dread going home because it was always the same old questions "have you been skipping school? Your friends cannot be trusted, you have a boyfriend."

Fatima and Yasmin changed. They became more like my parents; the way in which my father treated them was beginning to repeat on us. Fatima would push my mother into thinking the worst; she poisoned my mother's mind and turned her against us. I used to try my very best to forget everything that went on at home, I used to switch off as soon as I got home from school. At times it was unbearable and I locked myself in the bathroom and try to cut myself with a razor or something sharp to take the pain away. But I had no peace, my mother or my sisters would bang on the door wanting to know why I was in there and how long I had been in the bathroom for. There was nowhere for me to escape to.

After my father's death, Fatima had a change of heart about her husband Kamran and reluctantly called him over to England. She said it was what father wanted and for my mother's sake as she felt they needed an older male figure in the family for security. Fatima went on another visit to Pakistan to finalise the documents for Kamran's visa application.

On her return she became pregnant and had her first child, a beautiful baby girl called Saba. Fatima was not happy because, like my parents, she also wanted a boy. She was also jealous because Shazia had another child and this time it was another boy, his name was Ali. She hated Shazia for it. Shazia was forced to feel that she was not wanted in the family, she was constantly told by Fatima she had no right coming to the house, that she had her own family to take care of, nothing else was of her concern. Shazia was heartbroken; like the rest of us she had lost a father and now Fatima told her that our mother had other concerns and did not need her help in any way.

During this time, Yasmin decided to change the way she dressed, she started wearing a head scarf and was reading about Islam a lot more. She had suddenly changed and wanted to become a traditional Islamic woman. She had graduated from college with flying colours and decided to go to university. My mother did not like the idea of her going to university but she changed her mind due to Fatima's influence; they were as thick as thieves.

Yasmin refused to call her husband Arshad over from Pakistan and she wanted a divorce. My mother was in tears as it was her brother's son. Both our families were torn apart.

For years, Arshad would not give her a divorce because he still wanted to come to England and Yasmin was his ticket to get here. Yasmin demanded that she would get a divorce and went to seek professional Islamic advice but she was told it was going to be a very long and painful process. The problem was that Yasmin married in Pakistan. She was struggling to get an Islamic divorce which was the correct way of separating and in Pakistan she was told the law always favours the man. She had filed for a divorce in England and it was granted but she still needed an Islamic divorce.

Fatima's husband Kamran came over from Pakistan. He was

very quiet but always did what he was told by his wife. But things soon changed. Like Kabir, he wanted to live a life of luxury and did not lift a finger to help with day to day tasks. He had no intention of learning English, and like Kabir he was also struggling to find a job.

Letters soon arrived from Pakistan as Kamran's family wanted money to be sent over. This caused endless arguments in Fatima's marriage. Fatima was subjected to violence from Kamran. He was a lot taller than her and much stronger. He would beat her constantly until she gave in to his demands. The rest of our family would try to intervene but we were always pushed aside.

On one occasion he had her pinned to the ground and I heard her screams from my bedroom, below hers. I rushed into her room and tried to get him off her. He turned towards me and punched me straight in my face. As a result I had a black eye and a broken nose. Fatima begged me not to call the police and said to me "think of my daughter" so, reluctantly I decided not to. The violence did not stop.

Kamran finally got himself a job in a take-away making pizzas in the evenings. He was secretly saving extra money as well as the money he had from Fatima and kept it locked away in his wardrobe. She became suspicious of him as he asked for more money from her; his excuses were "I am saving up for some new clothes" or "I am getting Saba some new toys." Fatima found his stash of money and banked the whole lot in the building society. Kamran learned about what she had done and hit the roof. This time she had a severely bruised back and she refused to go into hospital. She was in pain for days and slept downstairs as she could not walk anywhere.

He was always very apologetic after he hurt her and said she had pushed him to it. Fatima always said to me that she did not love Kamran and love was not everything in a relationship but she was only with him for her daughter's sake.

Fatima was seen as the bad person in Kamran's family's eyes, she did not get on with his brother's wives as they saw Fatima as being the one that controlled Kamran's life. She would not give into their demands. Kamran's family were very close and all lived together under the same roof in Pakistan. He had three other brothers who were all married and had lots of children, he also had two sisters with children of their own.

My mother grew to dislike Kamran as he always spoke back to her and disrespected her. She was ready to throw him out but she felt she had to let him be for Fatima's sake. But things were getting worse, he was disrespecting my mother more and more. She eventually cracked and told Fatima and Kamran to move out. Fatima brought herself a house and was really sad to leave.

Because of what was going on at home, my school work had suffered a lot. Aisha and I could not do much of our homework at home because we had to do cooking and cleaning. Our mother said that cooking was very important because our future husbands would need to be fed. So we did our homework whenever we got time at school.

8 I just want to be a teenager

A FEW YEARS had passed and things did not change. We were teenagers and we wanted to live like teenagers. We were not allowed to see our friends outside of school hours; the family would worry that we were out meeting boys. This mistrust meant that we also missed out on many school trips and activities. We hated being controlled like this.

Yasmin knew all about this and used it to build shadows of doubt in my mother's mind.

If we did not agree with anything or refused to do something were told that we were possessed or that someone had performed black magic on us. Fatima and Yasmin would then go with my mother to visit a holy woman who in their eyes was the chosen one that could reverse spells and change destiny.

Fatima was trying for another child but was unable to conceive. Going to the holy women gave her some sense of reassurance. She was very superstitious; she believed that relatives in Pakistan were jealous of our family and were trying to harm her, cause arguments between her and Kamran and break up her marriage.

My mother and sisters returned home with holy water and a verse from the Quran, written on soluble paper. They made Aisha and I drink it all so that the badness could be purged from our bodies. We were also told to wear a taweez around our necks - a black cord necklace with a verse from the Quran bound into it that was supposed to heal us.

My brother Abdul used to provoke my mother into hitting us, he knew how to push her buttons. If we wanted to do something or we needed money for some new shoes we would ask him to speak to our mother. He was always referred to as my father, my mother used to say he looks and acts just like him.

Abdul always found his way into our room if Aisha and I wanted peace and quiet. He would come up on purpose to annoy us and he would try his very best to get involved in our conversations. He did not have many friends and he loved being the centre of attention at home.

On one occasion, our teacher had organised a trip to Disneyland Paris; we really wanted to go and it was a weekend trip so we wouldn't be missing any school days. We were too afraid to ask our mother because we knew the answer would be no. So Aisha and I asked Abdul to put a good word in and try to persuade mother to let us go. He wanted us to beg him and plead with him. At first we refused, but we really wanted to go on this trip with all our friends and so reluctantly we surrendered to his demands. He went away to speak with our mother and shortly afterwards we were told that we could go.

On this trip we wanted to wear trousers and not salwar kameez because all of our friends were going to wear Western clothing. My mother would not allow it as it showed too much freedom. She said people would talk and say "look at those girls, their father has just passed away and look at them now doing what they want, destroying their father's reputation - their mother is letting it happen." We knew she was not going to change her mind so we came up with a compromise. At that time there was a trend where girls would wear loosely fitted trousers that looked like a salwar and a skirt was attached over it so it looked like a salwar kameez. For the top we brought a plain, loosely fitted top. This was the nearest we could get to wearing Western clothing.

Like Yasmin, Aisha and I started wearing make-up secretly because most of the girls at school were. We would take some to school with us, wear it on the bus and untie our hair. On the way home from school we would take it all off on the bus and tie our hair back up again just in case someone saw us. We would then hide our make-up in our shoes or anywhere we knew our sisters or mother would not look and find it.

During the following year we received endless calls and letters from relatives in Pakistan asking for our hand in marriage. My mother would turn them all down and say "the girls are too young, when they finish school that will be the right time for offers."

At school, Aisha and I had the same friends; we always did ever since we were in primary school. Our school friends were very bubbly, the way they spoke made me think their parents were very easy going. Sannah, my best friend was the only child in her family. Her mother and father were both British born. She was allowed to have a mobile phone and she told me that her parents would never force her into an arranged marriage. I used to envy her because I knew my future was already planned for me. Sannah had high hopes for what she wanted to do after she left school, whereas I knew I had to get married and there would be no further education for me.

Aisha and I had such a laugh with our friends at school but we used to switch off the moment we came home. Between friends we would chat about almost anything, we felt our friends were more like the sisters we never had.

Shackled to my Family

9   Mother's death

MOTHER BECAME ILL. Over the following few months she had various scans at the hospital and she grew worse day by day. Aisha and I were still at secondary school and we were preparing for our mock exams. Our younger brothers and sisters were at primary school.

My mother went into hospital for an operation to remove some gallstones but when she was operated on what the doctors found was not gallstones but cancer. She had developed pancreatic cancer and it was progressing fast. My mother had chemotherapy to kill off the cancerous cells and it looked like the treatment was working.

Eventually she was allowed back home but she had to be bedridden. She had lost a lot of weight and looked like a shadow of her former self. She became very distant, she would hardly talk but when she did it was always in riddles. She would say "remember who your father was, remember who your family is and what they mean." She was convinced we were out to destroy the family's good name. Even when she was ill she still put the family's reputation before everything else.

My mother's treatment was not working. She was constantly in and out of the hospital. She refused to go into the Douglas Macmillan care centre as she wanted to be with her family. She could not speak a word of English so she expressed her feelings and emotions to the doctors through us.

She was adamant that she wanted to stay at home and not to be in a nursing home. My mother had no love left in her. All I wanted from her was to show some love towards us. We were her daughters, we had done nothing wrong. For years I used to feel like killing myself and wished I was born into a different family and be loved for who I was.

While my mother was in hospital we were still attending school and it felt like we were no longer being watched all the time. Fatima and Yasmin were always at the hospital while the children were at school - we had a bit of freedom to do what we wanted. Aisha and I started to have our friends call us at home, we used to watch television and go to bed when we wanted to.

Due to my mother's illness Yasmin gave up University partway through. She had to devote her time to my mother's needs because Fatima had her own commitments. During this time, my mother's treatment had stopped working completely; she took a turn for the worse and was taken back into hospital. She never recovered.

The doctors told us that the cancer had spread, that she would not recover and she would die. I felt so useless. I wanted to help her, I wished I would die instead of her. I felt like my heart had sunk. She was still my mother and there was nothing that I could do to make her better. The whole family was told not to tell my mother anything more about her illness. Looking back I feel she already knew.

Aisha and I had time off school, we did not complete any of our mock exams. The rest of the children were sent to school as there was no one to look after them. I remember the last day in which I saw my mother fully wake. I was about to leave the hospital after staying there for most of the day. She pulled at my arm and called me over and said "make sure you listen to your sisters and do what they say." She said it in such a forceful way, there was no love in her eyes. I just walked away thinking this was the same old stuff that I was used to hearing.

The following day her condition worsened and she fell into a coma. The doctors and nurses told us there was nothing they could do except to make her comfortable. She had stopped eating and was being fed through a tube. Her condition was like this for weeks.

My mother was visited by relatives that wanted to see her. My father's older sister who we did not get along with also came to the hospital on a number of occasions. She was about seventy years old and was always so over the top with her reactions.

This particular time which always sticks in my mind was when she saw my mother in a frail condition and automatically assumed she had died. She started howling and crying like she was possessed, she started praying and reciting verses from the Holy Quran. Everyone was so shocked and asked her to calm herself down as my younger sister Nadia was by my mother's beside and did not know that my mother was going to die. Fatima and Yasmin felt she was too young to understand.

Days had gone by and there was no change in my mother's condition; we used to try to speak to her and tell her what we had done that day, in the hope of getting a reply or even a nod. A few days later we were at the hospital again and we were told by a nurse that mother was not responding to anything and that her heart had become really weak. We were told she could pass away at any moment. All of the family gathered at the hospital by her bedside except for the children - they were cared for by a relative. We were all gathered for hours, it felt like a lifetime.

Hours passed by and soon the curtains in my mother's room were drawn. My mother was being given a bed bath by one of the nurses; this was done on the instruction of my sister Fatima. She said to me at the time this is a ritual that Muslims do when someone is about to pass away. I could not control my tears any longer and left quickly for the nearby toilet.

On my return, my sisters had brought a holy women to the hospital, the same one which my sisters were seeing on a regular basis. Her intentions were to help the spirit release itself from the body quickly and painlessly. She had prepared my mother and I noticed that my mother's feet were bound together by her big toes. The woman was sitting by my mother's beside in a emotionless state holding the Holy Quran in one hand and some holy water in the other. Everyone else was in floods of tears and repeating everything that the holy-women was saying as she splashed the water across my mother's body. All of a sudden the holy women stopped. She said that my mother had gone to a better place. We were all overcome with sadness and could not control our cries. Fatima was hysterical, I had never seen her like that before, she was howling uncontrollably and was forced to stop her cries by the nurses because she was disturbing other patients.

The following few hours were the worst I had felt in a long time, I did not know how to feel, I could not cry any longer; my tears had dried up. My mother had just died and I felt a sense of relief. She was no longer in pain and I no longer had to be scared. Soon the undertakers arrived with a black body bag. They took my mother's body to the mortuary and all of my mother's belongings were gathered together for one last time.

The room inside the hospital seemed ghostly. The bed was remade and it looked as though my mother had never been there and nothing had happened the night before. Everything was ready for the next patient.

Leaving the hospital was very strange; it felt like we had been living there. I remember looking at strangers and thinking why are you not sad? I felt like time had come to a standstill, like in a dream and I was going to wake up soon. Arriving home also seemed strange as there were people arriving every couple of minutes paying their respects and telling me how sorry they were to hear of our loss.

The house was pulled apart; all of the furniture was removed and the living room was empty. People were sitting on the floor praying for my mother's spirit.

Fatima and Yasmin were organising the funeral, they had gone shopping an hour earlier for food as people were coming in and staying for hours and needed to be fed. Aisha and I were told to wash ourselves properly and start to pray for our mother's soul.

Soon after, the house was filled with people. The men were directed to a different room by my brother-in-law Kamran and the women were all sent to the living room. Most of the people there were not family members, the vast majority of our relations were living in Pakistan. I remember being pulled from one person to another and each giving me a kiss or a cuddle. I did not know who these people were but they thought very highly of my mother. I remember feeling really loved at this time because I was constantly asked if I was ok or if I needed something or if I wanted to talk. This was all very new to me because I was used to just keeping everything locked away inside and not talking about how I was feeling.

Aisha and I stayed together during this tough time, we kept an eye on Laila and Nadia as they were very young and they needed to know that they were not alone.

That night we were too afraid to sleep upstairs so all of us including Shazia and her children and a few of my cousins all slept on the living room floor. I remember feeling really excited as we had never had our cousins sleep over before, we never had any sleep-overs when we were children.

My cousins were my mother's sister's daughters. Their names were Uzma and Sophia. Uzma was older than Sophia and was married happily to her first cousin. Sophia had a daughter called Salma and was married to Kamran's younger brother Imran. Both sisters had an arranged marriage but Sophia was not happy, having been forced into her marriage and had never been back to Pakistan.

Sophia refused to call her husband over from Pakistan as she said she was not happy in her marriage and did not love him. For years she was hounded by Imran's family. Sophia's daughter was eight years old and she resembled her father. Both Uzma and Sophia were quite westernised; they wore trendy clothes and always looked really nice. Their mother had died quite a few years earlier and their father was not strict at all - they had the freedom to do what they wanted.

Their father, uncle Naveed remarried a few years later after the death of his wife. He remarried to someone a lot younger than himself in Pakistan. Uncle Naveed was in his sixties and his wife in her early twenties. He was having trouble getting a visa for his wife, he had been told by immigration that she could not possibly be his wife because she was too young and she looked more like his daughter than anything.

Uzma and Sophia were very angry with their father, they felt he was acting like a child and that he had been brainwashed when he went to Pakistan. Uzma and Sophia felt like this woman had tricked him into marriage and that there was no love involved. The woman just wanted to come to England.

I got on really well with Sophia and I enjoyed talking to her. She was more on my wavelength. Uzma was a lot different to Sophia, she was not as outgoing or loud as her sister and she always behaved in a mature manner which made her seem a lot older.

The following day was very much the same. People came to the house to pay their respects. That particular day was when my mother's body was to be brought to the house for one last time. Before this, seven women were chosen to help wash and purify my mother's body before the funeral. I put myself forward because I wanted to be a part of this as I felt I could be closer to her. The body was at a local mosque where we were able to wash her and recite verses from the Holy Quran.

That evening my mother's body was taken to the house because Fatima and Yasmin felt that she should be at home for one last night. The body was in a wooden casket and my mother's face was visible through the glass window. She was moved into the centre of the living room where we were able to see her and pray. I remember looking at her and thinking she was just asleep and she was going to wake up soon.

That day we spent hours praying. The day seemed so long and that night we kept the body at the house and stayed up and prayed once more. We were too afraid to sleep upstairs because of the body being in the house. I could not sleep near the coffin; I was so scared of being left alone with the body or leaving the room and going to a different room in the house. I felt like my mother's presence was with me at all times and she was watching my every move.

Fatima and Yasmin were not very approachable during my mother's death. They seemed very distant and would not come and comfort us or receive comfort from us, I felt like we were alone. Shazia was different, she would come over and see how everyone was and comfort us. She was very concerned for all of us and really helped me come to terms with our mother's death. Nadia was very young, she would not stop crying; all she wanted was my mother. Looking at Nadia would make everyone cry.

The following morning was the day of the funeral. This was going to be the last day we ever saw our mother. My mother's body was to be taken to the mosque later that afternoon and then flown to Pakistan. We were not asked if we wanted our mother to be buried in Pakistan our opinion did not count because our parents' wishes were to be buried in Pakistan with the rest of the family. The time came when my mother's body was leaving and never returning. Everyone crowded round the coffin and said their goodbyes. I remember being pushed aside by Fatima because she did not want to let go of the coffin, she was crying uncontrollably and did not want anyone to take the body away. Eventually she was forced to move out of the way. I always felt Fatima liked the fact that she was made a fuss of by other people and she wanted the attention, she would not show us any love.

The males of the family took the body to the mosque for the funeral prayer. Yasmin, Kamran and Abdul would be accompanying the body to Pakistan.

10 Back to reality

BACK HOME, A feast was being prepared for the funeral. Everyone helped prepare the food. I remember feeling all of this would be over soon and things would be back to normal, except of course, my mother would not be there. I was not looking forward to reality sinking in.

The house after the funeral was very quiet, there were fewer people coming to the house now. Fatima changed yet again and she became a lot more approachable; she would do her best with everyone because she was on her own as Kamran had gone to Pakistan. The house was even quieter at night - we were afraid to sleep in our own rooms so we all slept together in one room.

Fatima told us stories to take our mind off being scared. She would tell us about her childhood. I had never heard her stories and I had never seen that side of her before. One particular story which she made me promise not to repeat to anyone was that she had a crush on an English man (a non-Muslim) when she was in her teens. Our family was living in a different house at the time - Aisha and I were only toddlers back then.

This man was our neighbour and he too liked Fatima very much. Fatima fell in love with him but could not do anything about it because our father was so strict and she was always afraid of him.

She said she would go outside and hang the washing out just to see him. She said that he thought she was very beautiful. She went on, saying that our father was getting suspicious because this man was always out in the garden whenever Fatima would be hanging the washing out. So he stopped her going outside or he would go out with her. She said she used to cry herself to sleep and wished things were different, that our parents were not so strict and she wished she could have dated this man. I went on to ask her if she could have stood up to our father or ever say anything to him. She said he would have killed her. I was beginning to see a side to her that I really liked.

Every week we would get a phone call from Yasmin. She would ask how everyone was and she would tell us how everyone in Pakistan was. She went on to say our mother was buried alongside our father and that the second funeral in Pakistan went well.

She also told us that she had fallen in love with someone over there. We were very happy for her as she always felt she would never find anyone. She told us that she had fallen for Imran, Sophia's husband and the father of Salma. We were all stunned to hear the news. Fatima was not happy, she said that Yasmin had been brainwashed and that Kamran and his family were to blame. Fatima felt like Kamran had planned the whole thing to get his brother over to England. She knew that Imran was desperate to come to England and that Sophia knew he would go to any length to get his visa.

Yasmin and Fatima were not seeing eye to eye; they would give each other abuse over the phone and Fatima's marriage was on the line. She was threatening to divorce Kamran if he helped in any way.

Weeks had gone by and Aisha and I were due to start school again. We were in our final year of secondary school. Going back to school after such a long time was very difficult. We were trying to make things as normal as possible.

Weeks later, Yasmin, Kamran and Abdul were back from

Pakistan. They had brought back lots and lots of presents. Yasmin was pushing Imran into getting a divorce from Sophia, Sophia agreed but said she did not want Imran to have anything to do with his daughter Salma. Yasmin was not speaking to Sophia and she hated her name being mentioned. Fatima eventually changed her mind about Imran and was happy for them both.

Soon, the house was full again and Fatima had moved back into her own house. Yasmin had custody of all of us - she had inherited all of my parents' assets until my brothers were old enough and agreed to my parents' wishes to have an arranged marriage. The rest of us did not receive any inheritance; we were always told "mother and father wanted everything to be left to Abdul and Hamid."

Once everything was settled down and we were all back at school the letters from Pakistan started coming in again. This time it was from relatives that did not normally send letters. There were wedding proposals for Aisha and I. I remember feeling we were being discussed and our lives were being made for us. Yasmin and Fatima would take the decision upon them to say who they felt the right person was for us, we were left in the dark.

Every day Aisha and I were the hot topic in the house. Abdul knew that we did not like it, he used to push the conversation and sit back and enjoy the arguments. His marriage was also discussed but he would always say "Aisha and Samina are getting married first."

Going to school was the only place where we could get any peace; we started to feel a lot braver at standing up for ourselves. We used to have our hair down for school or wear a little make-up and when we were questioned at home we would say "You used to do the same thing when you were at school" and then the questioning would stop. Yasmin would try to control us as much as she could; she used to go through our things and try to get anything to prove that she was right. She would hit us and make us feel worthless. She would also hit Laila and Nadia because she felt she had the power to do so. Laila and Nadia would do nothing but take the punishments. Aisha and I took it upon ourselves to look out for our two younger sisters. We felt like they had been through enough and we did not want the same things that happened to us when we were younger to happen to them. Yasmin hated that; she would hit me but I would hit her twice to prove she cannot hurt me and get away with it. Soon she learned that I was not having any of it. But still we felt that the arranged marriage was going to happen because we were emotionally blackmailed into thinking this was what mother and father would have wanted and that we will be disgracing their good name and the reputation of our entire family.

At school, some of our friends were in the same situation; they knew they too would be having an arranged marriage sometime in their lives. We would always say to our friends "none of you can come to our weddings because it will be in Pakistan." we did not have any relatives our age in England.

Yasmin and Fatima would always say we were ugly and that we would never have any man look at us anyway. I hated looking in the mirror because I did not see myself as being attractive. I had a lot of teenage spots on my forehead which made my lack of confidence even worse.

11 Going to Pakistan

AISHA AND I were working towards our GCSEs. We had weeks left before we finished school for good. Yasmin and Fatima were discussing arrangements for who was going to go to Pakistan that year. Plans were being made and it was decided that Aisha and I were going along with Fatima, Kamran, and their daughter Saba. We had our suspicions about why we were going straight after school, we were told it was time we paid our respects and saw our parents' graves, so we agreed.

It was a hot summer's day, we had finished our exams and it was our last day of school. We were going to our local town for lunch and wanted to take some pictures. Yasmin and Fatima assumed it was a full day at school and we were told to go straight home from school but we never did.

That day we had a great time; we travelled by bus to town with our friends, it was full of laughs - we talked about what we had done over the past five years and how different we are as people now. When we went back home we were asked what we did that day and Yasmin wanted to see the pictures. I told her that my camera had broken and that my friend Alina had taken the pictures.

Aisha and I had the same friends at school; we both were really sad because most of our friends were going to different colleges and we would never see them again. Fatima and Yasmin would never allow us to go out socialising with our friends and only way we could keep in contact would be if they went to the same college as us.

Soon it was time for the trip to Pakistan. We were going to see our parents' grave and pay our respects. I had my passport renewed because I had not visited Pakistan since I was a little girl.

The day came when we were leaving for Pakistan, we were dropped off at the airport by Kamran's friend - he was a taxi driver. Like Kamran, he was from Pakistan but the difference between them was that Kamran could not drive, he never learnt to. His friend like many other Pakistani men would drive taxis to earn a living. This was an easier job for them because they did not really need any qualifications to drive apart from knowing the local area.

During the ride to the airport Kamran asked Aisha and I if we were excited. Our reply was that we were, but a bit nervous at the same time. He said our relatives in Pakistan were counting the hours and they could not wait to see us. He said his family would look after us very well.

The airplane journey was very long. This time we went on a Pakistani Airline called PIA. The plane was filled with Pakistani people - I remember thinking I had not seen so many Pakistani people since I had attended a wedding a few years earlier. I was getting restless by the time the plane finally landed at Islamabad airport. As we all made our way to the platform, Kamran told Aisha and I to put our scarves over our heads. My reply in return was "no". Fatima was quick to intervene by saying "Do as you are told, you do not walk around here without a head scarf, what will people think of you? You are a Muslim girl, think of your parents' reputation, you are not in England now!" I could not believe what I was hearing, my opinion did not count.

Kamran and Fatima both wanted Aisha and I to adapt to their way of life. I remember thinking I was not born in

Pakistan, I was a British Pakistani so why was I forced to wear a head scarf. I didn't wear a head scarf in England, so why should I change when I am in Pakistan? All these questions, thoughts and much more were going through my mind. Aisha's views were the same but like myself she knew there was nothing that we could do but to agree with everything that we were told to do. I wanted to react but I did not want to make a scene. I knew nobody would take our side, we were just two people stuck in an Islamic country.

Shortly after, we were greeted by Kamran's brother Imran and his father Farooq, my uncle. There were a few more people there but I did not recognise them. I asked Fatima who they were, she said they were our cousins and the reason why I could not remember was because I was very young when I first saw them. There were endless tears as we were greeted. The tears were mainly for my parents. I remember saying to Aisha "why all the drama?" People were starting to stare as Fatima began to cry uncontrollably. The temperature was reaching the mid-forties and the heat was overwhelming but that did not stop our relatives hugging us and pulling us from person to person.

We eventually left the airport and made our way outside. I was shocked to see so many poor people, most of whom had no shoes on. The people were referred to as "beggars" by my relatives. Uncle Farooq shooed them away. He said to us all "do not have any pity on these people, they are merely beggars" I really did pity them, I wanted to help them but I was forced to walk away quickly. We were all told to keep our belongings close to us, so we did.

Uncle Farooq brought along a local villager who could drive to take us back to the village in his people-carrier. The ride to the village where we were staying was not as bad as I remembered from the first time. There were more roads now than I first remembered and more houses had been built.

Half way through the journey, the driver stopped for a break at a local town. As he went to refresh himself we all stretched our legs and were stopped by some local people selling drinks and food. We were all very thirsty and we longed for a cold, iced drink. Aisha and I had no money on us, we were not given any by Fatima. So Aisha asked Fatima if we could buy a drink from one of the people, Fatima said yes and was about to go into her purse and get some rupees out when Kamran stopped her and said "It is a waste of money, why don't you wait a few hours, we will be home soon" Fatima started shouting at Kamran, she knew he was very tight-fisted when it came to spending money. Fatima ignored what Kamran said and brought us some drinks.

The journey took about four hours. We eventually arrived at the village and were greeted by some children who had run quite a distance after seeing us from the roof of their home. The children were Kamran and Imran's nieces and nephews. I could not help but stare at them, they were so very thin, their frames just skin and bone. All of the children wore salwar kameez but I was shocked to see that some of them had no shoes on their feet, they looked so poor. My first impressions were not what I expected.

The children were more than happy to carry our luggage because they wanted to know if we had brought them any presents. Fatima told Aisha and I to keep our bags and carry them ourselves; she knew from past experience that our belongings were not our own once we got inside the house.

The house looked very much the same as it did nine years ago, but the differences being that there was now a toilet and a shower. There were fewer animals but the family was much bigger than I remembered.

The house was divided into two. The first half was home to my elder uncle Farooq, his wife Shaheen, and their daughter Nazia, sons Imran, Nazeer, and Yaser. Nazeer had no children and Yaser was the elder son, he had four children.

Nazia was married to the son of another of my uncles on my

father's side. She was married to uncle Aslam's son in Lahore but he did not like her so she went back to live with her family.

The second half of the house was where my younger uncle Ahmed lived with his wife Miriam, their children Nasreen and Bushra. Kabir who also lived there was married to my Sister Shazia. Bushra was married to Nazeer and Nasreen was married to Yaser.

We spent the rest of the day talking mainly about my parents and how they were missed terribly. My Aunty Miriam was overwhelmed with emotion, she just wanted to hug and kiss Aisha and I. She said being close to us meant she was close to my parents.

After what had seemed a very long day, Aisha and I really wanted to see where our parents were buried. We had heard so much about the graveyard and what a lovely burial site it was. So Imran took Fatima, Aisha and I to the local cemetery where my parents and family members were buried.

The cemetery was about a twenty minute walk from the house. When we got there we noticed that our parents were buried alongside my father's parents. My mother's parents were not buried there because they came from a different village and so were buried there. My father's grave had a marble surrounding with verses from the Holy Quran on it.

My mother's grave did not have anything on it. Imran said that the earth had not set and that the grave itself was wet due to the monsoon weather. If anything was to be done with it, the grave would simply sink.

Imran said the marble headstone had been ordered but Fatima was furious, she had previously sent money over to Kamran's family for my mother's grave. She felt like they did not care. She had to be calmed down by Imran because she was cursing and it was seen to be inappropriate at a grave yard.

Before we got to the cemetery we prepared ourselves for praying. We had to cover ourselves from head to toe and we took a Holy Quran with us. As Muslims, we were told that praying for someone who had passed away does their soul good and helps them get to paradise quickly. I really wanted that for our parents even though most of the time I hated them and wished I was born into a different family. They were still my parents and nothing could change that. Being near them at the cemetery was very scary. I felt afraid, like my parents were watching me and in my mind I thought they were not happy with me and the way I had been behaving.

On the way home I asked Fatima how she felt and she said she felt at ease knowing that our parents were both buried together. She said that praying helped her a lot because she was doing something good for them. Aisha felt the same as me, she also felt praying was a good way of doing something good for them. But why did I feel different? I thought being close to them would help me realise that they had passed away and all the thoughts and nightmares that I was having would go away.

Back at the house everyone was getting ready for the evening meal. Both families had prepared their own food. We were given a choice of both. The meal was not quite what I expected. Even though the house was one, I could see a clear divide between both families. They ate separately and did not share their food with each other. I felt like there was a rivalry between them both.

When I was eating my meal I had to go to the other side of the house if I wanted to taste some of their food. When I got to the second half of the house - Uncle Armed's half - I was asked by Nasreen whose meal I preferred? I found that very strange as she was married to Yaser but she did not eat with him or sleep in the same half of the house as him. I was beginning to see that their marriage was not what I called a marriage, I felt it was only to unite the two families but there was no unity.

It was early and the two families were preparing for sleep, I was not tired as I had caught up on my sleep earlier in the plane.

I asked Bushra, one of my cousins, if there was a television that we could watch. She said there was only one, a very small black and white one. I did not see a television in either house. She told me uncle Farooq had locked it away because watching television is "bad" and girls especially do not watch it. She said if you ask him he may allow it because you are from England and it is allowed over there. I remember thinking if you can't watch television what else can you do around here? So I asked uncle Farooq, he said yes but only for a short while because electrically was expensive. The electricity was on a meter and he said there are regular power cuts too.

So the television was switched on, but the station was switched to uncle Farooq's taste, a Pakistani soap opera based on army life. He found it his duty to tell me how interesting and wonderful it was. He said "you do not want to fill your mind with distasteful pop music or watch mind numbing soaps that destroy your mind", he also said "you will lose your sense of reality." I found that bit very amusing.

After about half an hour, the television was switched off. I asked Fatima if we could have a walk outside. It was not dark but I just wanted to see a bit more of the village. She said "No, because it is dangerous and no girls are allowed out in the evenings, even to the corner shop." So what was I supposed to do? I wanted to go to my room, but I did not have a room, none of us did. Everyone was going to sleep outside. The air was very humid, it was hot and sticky. Inside the house it was like a sauna. That night we slept on manji beds. These were traditional beds made from wood and plastic strips. The women and children slept on the ground floor and the men slept on the rooftops, with my Uncle Farooq sleeping near the front, guarding the house. He was keeping watch because during the night the houses would be robbed or people started fires. He was also on guard to try and keep away any "*giddar*" (jackals).

12   Could I live in Pakistan?

SLEEPING ON A manji was very uncomfortable I just could not get to sleep. Aisha was sharing the manji with me because there were not enough for everyone to have one each. The manji was not very big, you could say it was the same size as a single bed but without the comfort.

It was dark and I was afraid - I could not believe I was sleeping outside! I could hear noises, Mosquitoes were flying around me. I wanted to cover myself, to hide but it was very warm. I could hear cries, I wanted to believe it was a cat or something like that but my mind was telling me otherwise. I could only think about ghosts.

Back in England, Shazia would tell me that Bushra was possessed by a ghost-like spirit, a bad spirit. This ghost was with her at all times. Bushra was sleeping two beds down from me. I was too afraid to open my eyes and take a look. The sound was coming from a far corner of the yard. I tried to wake Aisha but she got angry with me and said "just go to sleep!" But I couldn't, so I covered my head with my scarf that I was wearing and hoped I would fall asleep.

I was woken up at sunrise by the sound of water. Most of the adults were awake and washing themselves in preparation for the morning prayer. I was very tired because I did not get much sleep that night. I could hear the Imam at the village mosque reciting the call to prayer through a loudspeaker.

Nazia told Aisha and I to get up and start praying. When we refused she was shocked at us and began to give us a lecture. In our defence Aisha said "why are you forcing us to pray when Fatima is still asleep? She is the older one, the role model, shouldn't she be praying?" Nazia was surprised at Aisha's reaction and told us we were spoilt. Aisha and I went back to sleep.

A couple of hours later I was woken up once more but this time it was a rattling sound coming a few inches from me. It was Nazia she was doing the washing up. She was washing the dishes at the well next to where we were sleeping. She said to me "you must get up now it's time for breakfast." "Breakfast," I said "this early?" The time was 5.30 am. I could not believe the two families were awake and raring to go at such an early time of the morning. Reluctantly, I did what I was told.

My breakfast was not the usual kind that I was used to having back in England. There was no cereal or toast. Instead there was a Parata, this was a roti stuffed with potato and vegetables. The smell was overpowering, it smelt very greasy. Almost like a traditional English breakfast. Also I had an option of having some egg biscuits which I was not keen on. The soft texture of the biscuit dunked in tea made me feel sick. I ate the parata with a cup of traditional Pakistani tea which had aniseed and basil leaves in it. The milk that was used was goats milk which had its own distinctive taste.

While I was eating my breakfast one of Nareen's children threw themselves on me, this made me spill my tea. I remember thinking her kids were wild and needed to be taught some manners. Her children were very naughty and not the cleanest of children.

She had a young daughter, about seven years old. She constantly had a runny nose and ran around the place like a wild animal. The children rarely went outside, but when they did I heard from Fatima that it was quite embarrassing at times.

Before we had even finished our breakfast, there were people at the door. The people were villagers who came to say hello. I was dreading this part because I knew the hugs and the kissing were to follow again. The villagers were hot and sweaty, the temperature was rising and it was beginning to be a very warm day.

I was asked if I spoke any Mirpuri and I said I could but not very well. So they asked me what I thought about Pakistan so far. "Well," I thought… "Hmmm," I lied and said it was wonderful. It was only my first full day. I could not begin to imagine what the rest of the time was going to be like; we had another seven weeks to go. I really did not want to spend the majority of the time in the village. I thought the whole idea of visiting a different country was to travel a bit. So I hoped that was on the cards.

The house was filling up quickly with people who to me were total strangers. My parents were mentioned most of the time with the odd whisper from Fatima telling me to stay away from a certain person. I wanted to know why but she said "I will tell you later."

Aisha also wanted to explore. There was only so much we could do around the house. The house had around 12 bedrooms. It was an open plan house with stone pillars on the front and balconies around the entire house. Some people could say it was a mansion but a run down one. It reminded me of the houses that were built in ancient Greece. The house needed a lot of work doing to it. There were cracks in the walls, paint was stripping away from the walls, the doors would not shut properly, the ceiling fans were very noisy and most of which did not work. The bathroom was awful, it was like a big stone hut with a large tap inside that was used as a shower and there was no shower cubical. The water was always ice cold. If I wanted a hot shower I had to boil some water.

The toilet did not flush properly. There was a hole in the ground next to it which was also used as a toilet. The smell was horrendous! I was told the bathroom was an extension and it was built a few months earlier. There was no toilet before - everyone had to go outside in the fields. I remember thinking everyone was better off going to the fields because I could not take the smell any more.

The rooms were not bedrooms I could not see any beds that were made up. The manjis were used as beds and sofas - somewhere for people to sit on. The floor was stone, with broken tiles.

The windows had no glass, there were just window frames with bars inside to keep them stable. The windows had shutters that could be closed and locked. I was told that there was no need for glass in the windows because the weather is so hot in Pakistan. The windows that they have help the house cool down and during the winter the shutters are closed. I also asked why the walls were a mint green colour. I was told that green is a cooling colour.

Once Aisha and I had completed a tour of the house we sat on the roof for a few hours. From the roof we could see most of the village and beyond. I could see local village women taking their clothes to a small lake to wash. I could see some of the men in the fields cutting down sugar cane and planting. I could not see many local village children, they were all at school. Aisha and I were then joined by Nazia. She asked us what we were doing all by ourselves on the roof. We said we wanted to take a look at the village, but the only way we could do that was by sitting up here. Aisha went on by saying "Can we explore Pakistan a bit while we are here?" Nazia's reply was "Yes in a couple of weeks, you will be going to Lahore to see my sister" Nazia had another sister called Sameera; she was older than her and was married into a richer family. They were not complete strangers but distantly related.

We were very excited as this was a busy city and completely different to the village. Nazia took Aisha and I back downstairs because Fatima wanted to open her suitcases and give everyone their gifts. When Aisha and I got back downstairs, I could see an argument brewing between Nasreen and her mother-in-law Shaheen. They were jealous about each other's gifts. Nasreen was saying that Shaheen's clothes which Fatima had brought were a lot nicer than hers. She was shouting and saying, she always got things that were left overs that nobody wanted. I could not believe what I was hearing. I had heard stories back home in England that Nasreen was a very jealous and argumentative person. But what I could not understand was that my elder sister Shazia had sent plenty of gifts for Nasreen and her children because she was her sister-in-law. I felt that Nasreen was very ungrateful. Fatima did not have to give her anything but she did. I was beginning to know exactly what kind of a person Nasreen was and I did not like it one bit. I remember thinking I would go crazy living here.

13 A frightening experience

DAYS HAD GONE by and I was so bored. There was nothing to do around the house. All I could do was to make myself useful by helping to wash the dishes and carry out some cleaning. I felt like a village girl. I was hating my summer break.

Aisha and I wanted some new clothes because those that we had brought with us were not really right for summer's heat. So Kamran took Aisha and I along with Fatima and her daughter Saba to the local market. The market was a long distance from the village so we had to travel by horse and cart. Half way there we reached a very dangerous bridge. It was made from planks of wood, some of which were missing which meant that cars and vehicles could not travel over it. The horse and cart was the safest way.

Once we had passed the dreaded bridge we had to wait for a bus to take us to the market. While we waited for the bus I noticed that most of the women were accompanied by at least one male. I asked Fatima why this was. She said it was because women are not safe travelling on their own. Some men in Pakistan are capable of anything. I was very afraid as I looked around and saw gangs of men huddled together. I also noticed some men holding hands while they were walking. I started giggling as I turned to Aisha. She too saw what I was seeing and started giggling. I found it very strange because Aisha and I assumed the men were gay. In Islam this was forbidden. I asked Fatima why there were so many men that were holding hands, she said it was what the men did in Pakistan; it showed friendship. Strange, I thought.

As I looked around, I noticed some couples with children, well at least I thought they were couples. The male was walking a distance ahead of his wife, she was tagging along behind him with the children. As I started looking more and more I noticed a pattern. This time Kamran asked me what I was looking at, so I told him. He said "a man has a duty to walk a few steps in front of his wife and children." He said the male is always the head of the house. The husband always walks ahead of his wife.

"That's not fair" I said. He asked me why? I did not tell him my real opinion, which was men and women in England hold hands and that they are seen as equals. Instead I said to him "Islam says men and women are equal" Once I had said that, I was starting to feel afraid - I did not know what his reaction would be, as I felt the men were very strict here. Kamran seemed to ignore my answer and just walked away.

After a while, the bus turned up. There were quite a few people waiting for the same bus. Getting on the bus was a nightmare. There was no queue formed, people were just pushing and shoving each other trying to get on the bus. Kamran forced his way through and told us to get on quickly. When we got on the bus I saw there were two or three people per seat. The bus was three times more full than it should have been but the bus driver was still piling people on. People were on the roof of the bus, people were hanging on the side of the bus, people were squeezed on seats that were only meant for two people.

Kamran made sure that all of us females had a seat to sit on. Kamran was very protective. At one point I was asked by another female passenger to give up my seat for her son. Kamran got very angry and said to her "your son is a grown man, he should be ashamed of himself."

Eventually, the bus left for the market dangerously full.

The seats were very uncomfortable and there were no safety facilities on the bus, no emergency exit, all the exits were blocked by people. During the journey, the bus made regular stops to nearby villages to drop people off or pick up others.

While I was sitting on my seat with Kamran standing above like a bodyguard, I felt a hand grab my waist from the seat behind me. I quickly removed the hand and told Fatima what had just happened. She turned and looked around and saw a young man. She shouted at him and said "you should be ashamed of yourself, what if someone had done that to your sister?" He backed off. A few moments later I felt his hand again but he tried to grope my chest. I pulled his hand away and shouted to Kamran. Kamran was ready to kill this man. He could not believe he had the nerve to do such a thing. Kamran pulled him out of his seat and punched him a few times. The man was quick to disappear off the bus. I could not believe what had happened. Now I knew why women were not allowed to travel on their own.

We finally arrived at the market, it was very warm. All of the females had to cover their heads including me and we had to look respectable as Muslim women. The market was amazing, there were so many stalls selling clothing, jewellery, make-up and food. I felt dehydrated so I asked Fatima if we could stop for a drink she said yes, so we went to a stall and brought some fresh pineapple juice.

We then went to a clothing stall that looked like a giant tent. The stall had some amazing women's clothes. Some of which were ready made, the cloth was already sewn into a salwar kameez. Once we got inside the stall we were greeted by the stall holder. He was very quick in asking us if we wanted something to drink. Fatima said it was because he could tell we were from England, we asked for some juice. While we were looking at the clothes we were asked by various people who worked there if we wanted anything in particular. We said no but we did take a look at some very beautiful outfits.

Aisha and I chose some material that we liked, then all of a sudden Fatima was negotiating the price. After we had brought the material I asked her why she was haggling with the price, she said, "Once the stall people realise that you are from England the prices automatically shoot up because they think you have a lot of money and you haven't got a clue about the cost of things."

14   I cannot be myself

THAT NIGHT I found trying to sleep very difficult. All I could think about was what had happened that day. Thoughts were racing through my mind about what it must be like living day to day in Pakistan as a Muslim woman and my brief taster that very day. The whole time I was travelling from the village to the market I felt trapped - I could not be myself. Instead, I had to abide by the rules that were set by my relatives. Fatima constantly told me not to make eye contact with anyone. If you look at someone they will take it the wrong way. I asked her "The wrong way, How?" Her answer to me was, "Some people can curse you and put black magic on you. Or the men will assume you are giving them the eye, then come on to you." How very strange, I thought. I said to her "So am I to close my eyes when I am walking?" She just laughed at me.

The following morning, everyone was up at the crack of dawn again. Nobody ever seemed to have a lie in. Nazia, Nasreen and Bushra were cleaning the house again like slaves while the men just lay in front of the fans trying to cool themselves down. Nazia asked me to help her clean up again, she seemed to do that a lot. She would not ask anyone else to help her except me.

Nasreen and Bushra were cleaning their side of the house. This very morning I wanted to stand my ground and stop Nazia from taking advantage of me. So I stood up for myself and said "No." Nazia started shouting at me and saying "You

73

have changed! You are not the same girl that came here all those weeks ago." She was right, I wasn't. I did not want to be a slave to the men of the household, I did not want to spend my day cleaning up after them. That was all Nazia seemed to do. She used to wake up early and wash their clothes at the lake, then she would come home, cook breakfast, clean up after them again then spend her time doing household chores. I was not expecting Nazia to make a scene but she did. She began to cry and started sobbing to her mother. Her mother then said to me "Why are you picking on my daughter? She has been through such a lot."

I was not picking on her. I told her I did not want to clean up after anyone any more. I felt the only way that Nazia ever got noticed was by making a scene. She lost lot of confidence after she married her first cousin and went to live with him in a different part of Pakistan.

While she was over there she was treated very badly by her husband. He used to beat her and treat her like a slave. The last time she was there she was so badly beaten that he had broken one of her front teeth and the other top teeth were blackened through nerve damage. She was teased by the kids and she thought she was very ugly. Right from the very start I tried to help her because I could see how busy she was. So I tried to make her life easier by helping her do the washing and cleaning. I wished I hadn't bothered. Nobody was there to defend me, not even Fatima; she was my sister but instead she took her sister-in-law's side. Aisha said to me "We are outsiders here." I knew what she meant by this because we were British and not Pakistani born.

Aisha and I were never allowed to have any time to ourselves. If we did we would have Nazia or the children interrupting us. We had no privacy, there was no such thing in that house. I felt like I was going mad. Everywhere we went we would have someone with us or tagging along. Our belongings were not our own. I caught a few of the children on a number of occasions looking in our suitcases and if we were to say something we would have the children's mother Nasreen shouting and making a scene.

Nasreen had so many children but she could not look after them all. Yaser was on leave from the army during this time. He would never spend time with them. Nasreen and Yaser would argue all the time about the children and he would say "The children are your responsibility, you are their mother, that is what you are here for." Back in England whenever we would get the news that Nasreen was pregnant again we used to laugh and say "Not again, does she not know what contraception is?" She would always fall pregnant whenever Yaser came home from the Army, it was a well-known joke. Nasreen was very stubborn; she had her parents wrapped round her little finger - especially her mother. Whenever there was an argument her mother would always be the first person in line ready to defend her.

Shackled to my Family

15 Marriage proposals

OVER THE NEXT few days Aisha and I were the centre of attention in our family. While we were staying over in the village we would have more and more relatives turning up on our doorstep. Things were starting to fall into place; questions kept on coming, like how old are you? Have you seen my son? He is very handsome, you would really get on, you would make a lovely couple, why don't you come and stay with us for a few days? These questions were from relatives that when my parents were alive did not want to know us. Fatima was not happy; she would say "They are like vultures." She was trying her very best to make Aisha and I think what bad people they were. I felt Fatima did this because she already knew who she wanted to be our future partners.

Aisha and I had a fair idea of how Fatima's mind worked. She took it upon herself to be the head of the house since our mother and father passed away. She always said that our mother's wishes were for her to decide who we married. During this time, my Aunty Noreen and her family were always at the house. She was married to my mother's younger brother Aqeel. They were a lovely family - very polite, my family thought the world of them. Uncle Aqeel had three sons and two daughters. The eldest son was married and lived in England with my cousin Uzma. The second eldest son, Faisal was not married, nor was the youngest son Bilal. The two daughters Sabeena and

Rabia were married. The youngest daughter Rabia was married to my father's elder sister's son in England.

Aunty Noreen was spending a lot of her time at the house; she was not the kind of person that talked about her sons to us but she did the opposite and talked to Fatima. One evening while we were eating our evening meal out in the yard, Fatima brought Faisal and Bilal's name into the conversation. Faisal's name was always mentioned in England. Fatima would tease Aisha and say "He is very handsome, so polite, he would take good care of you. He is just the person that you would want as a husband." I felt Fatima's first priority was Aisha when it came to deciding who would marry who because Fatima looked after Aisha when she was growing up and she felt Aisha was more of a daughter to her than a sister.

Faisal was a lot older than Aisha; he was more than ten years older. Aisha and I often wondered why he was not married. Over the years, I learned that in my family people tend to get married at an early age and Faisal was not very young. Fatima would say to Aisha, "Can you remember when you were younger, the first time you went to Pakistan on my wedding? Well he was the one that played with you a lot. He would read to you and stuff." I remember thinking that was really disgusting because she was only nine at the time. Both families must have been discussing their possible marriage right from the start.

Later that evening I asked Aisha what she thought, she said she was not happy, she could not remember him. She hated the fact that she was constantly teased about him. Aisha had not seen Faisal now that she was a young girl. All she knew was what the family were telling her, they said he was tall and handsome with very fair skin. The fair skin bit was seen to be very nice; if you were blessed with fair skin people thought you were beautiful, good looking.

The following day Aisha was to meet Faisal for the very first time since she was a child. That morning she was teased by most of the family and they were saying "Both of you will look like a Bollywood couple, oh he is so handsome." The family were already discussing what their children would look like. Aisha was very nervous, I was too.

Faisal came to the house at about lunch time after the afternoon prayer. He arrived at the house with his mother. Aisha was seated on a manji beside Fatima and I. Faisal was greeted with hugs and kisses by Aunty Shaheen and Aunty Miriam. Aisha said to me she felt sick to her stomach because she felt like she was on show, waiting to be approved by someone and this someone just happens to be Faisal, a middle-aged man. Aisha whispered to me "I bet in Fatima's mind she thinks we are already engaged!" She must have promised me to Faisal. Aisha, like me, hated our family's traditions and values.

Aisha was not allowed to talk to Faisal alone but only under supervision. So Nazia sat beside them both, giggling. She acted very strangely and made Aisha feel even worse. I watched from a nearby manji. I could see Aisha was feeling very awkward; she had never had any man approach her before. She did not know how to feel. I could see her playing with the end of her head scarf trying to control her nerves. After a few minutes Faisal came away from where Aisha was sitting and sat on the same manji as Fatima, this was my chance to speak to Aisha, so I was quick to move from my seat.

I asked her in English about Faisal and what she thought about him because Nazia was still there and her English was not very good. Aisha said she was not attracted to him; she also said he was too old. She did not know what to say to him as he was very quiet.

Soon we were joined by Fatima, she wanted to know what Aisha thought about him. Aisha said she did not like him. Fatima ignored her because she did not want to make a scene in front of Faisal and his mother.

Every day after that Faisal's name was brought up in

conversation. Marriage seemed to be the hot topic once more and sure enough Aisha was engaged to Faisal.

We were staying more and more at Faisal's house, his parents were being very generous. Bilal was beginning to appear a lot more. He was a similar age to me – just two years older. He studied at a local college and he too had high hopes of living in England.

He was of a very slim build, his complexion was darker than his brother Faisal's, but the thing that caught my eye most of all about him was his teeth. He had two very large front teeth - like a rabbit, with a big gap in between. I could not help but laugh whenever I saw him. I knew from the very first time I saw and spoke to him that I was not attracted to him. I knew whatever anyone would say to me the fact still remained.

On one occasion while we were staying at his house his elder sister Sabeena came over to me and said "Bilal is very clever, he is so bright, he has dreams of becoming a doctor you know." I remember thinking "Wow, is this supposed to impress me?" I felt so bitter, Sabeena was trying her very best to try and get me to marry her brother. She wanted both of us sisters to be married into her family.

A few times, Sabeena would ask me to go with her to the kitchen and help her cook. The cooking was just a way of trying to persuade me into making a decision. She would always ask me what I felt about her brother and my answer was always "He is a nice boy." This was not what she wanted to hear. She would send Bilal over to me while I was sitting down chatting to his nieces. I could see the desperation in her eyes; she wanted me to fall in love with Bilal. Sabeena would say to me "He really likes you, he has fallen for you." I would think to myself "Why doesn't *he* tell me that, he does not come across as shy to me?" In my mind I thought "Why do these people play with other people's lives like this?" I could not understand why Sabeena was so pushy. What was she going to gain out of all this? She had her own life. Then I thought - has her mother, Aunty Noreen put her up to this?

It was the last day at Uncle Aqeel's house. I was busy gathering all of my belongings from one of the rooms which was situated on the roof. While I was doing so I was stopped by Bilal, he had come up to the roof to talk to me. I was on my own, which made me think this was planned by Sabeena. Bilal confessed his undying love for me. He said he wanted to marry me. I was expecting this because I had heard so much from his sister Sabeena. I said to Bilal I did not have any feelings for him, he was not hearing what I was saying, instead he tried to hug me and he tried to kiss me. I pushed him away and ran downstairs.

When I got down to the yard, Fatima and Aisha were already down there with Imran by the door ready to take us back to his house. I ran and told Fatima what had happened. Fatima was furious and she felt the invitation from Aunty Noreen was all a plan to try to persuade me to marry her son. Aunty Noreen was so apologetic, she said she could not believe what her son had done and that she had no idea of what was going on.

Imran had travelled to the village on his motorbike so he had to make two trips to take us all home. Fatima told myself and Aisha to get on the motorbike and go back with Imran first so we did.

On Fatima's return to the house, she told Kamran and the others about what had happened. Uncle Farooq was furious, he was very angry with Uncle Aqeel and his family. Fatima was starting to question Aisha and Faisal's engagement. She started to question the whole family. She did not trust them as much as she did before. She told Kamran's family that she did have words with Aunty Noreen and Uncle Aqeel. She told them that there was no way I was to marry her son Bilal and that she was starting to think twice about Aisha's engagement.

Aisha saw me surrounded by the rest of the family and

she took her chance of taking me away from them all as she could see I was very much upset. Aisha led me to the bathroom which was the only place where we would not be disturbed. She asked me what had happened because she knew I had not spoken to anyone properly and no one was taking my feelings into consideration. All they were bothered about was what shame this could have caused. I told Aisha about how Bilal had confessed his undying love for me and how he had tried to kiss me. Aisha then asked me how I felt. I told her that I was afraid. I went on to say I was not afraid of Bilal but the thought of kissing him and I was afraid of him kissing me. Aisha started to laugh and in return made me laugh. As she laughed she said "Were you afraid of his teeth? I knew I would be." I pushed her to one side in a friendly way and said I was afraid in general, I had never been in that situation before and I did not want my first kiss to be with him because he meant nothing to me. I could see Aisha understood my point of view.

16 Aisha is engaged

THE NEXT FEW days were very busy while Aisha's engagement party was being organised. We only had two weeks left in Pakistan before we were due to fly back to England. Uncle Farooq was the person who made the final decision regarding Aisha's marriage after consulting with Fatima and Yasmin. He was the elder one, a father figure to us all since our father passed away. The word was quickly spread about the engagement between Aisha and Faisal and relatives were soon asking about me and if I was engaged.

We had heard a rumour that Aunty Noreen was telling people that I was engaged to her son Bilal - this was completely untrue! I was very pleased when the decision was made and I was not to marry him because I had no feelings for him nor was I the slightest bit attracted to him. Fatima had learned about what had happened, she was very angry, the whole family were.

Aunty Noreen apologised for what she had said and she knew she was in the wrong. She had hoped Fatima would have changed her mind and agree to the marriage. Aunty Noreen's motives were that she thought by telling people that I was engaged to her son this may keep possible proposals from relatives away and she was right, people did stay away. Fatima threatened Aunty Noreen by saying "If you lie again or push me into making any decision, the engagement between Aisha and Faisal will be broken." This was a real shock to her and she promised with her heart not to say another word.

Aisha did not have a big engagement party, mainly close relatives were invited. Money was a huge factor as Fatima said the wedding would cost a lot and there was no point in splashing out on the engagement. Lots and lots of gifts bad been bought for Aisha. Faisal's family were trying to impress ours by saying to Aisha "Don't be shy in asking for anything, we will buy you whatever you want." Aisha and I felt they were trying to buy her affections, so they flaunted gifts at her in the hope of making her feel happier. They could tell she was not happy and they were afraid their dreams would be shattered. Aisha had a pure gold Asian engagement ring that Faisal's family had given her. She was also given many beautiful clothes and accessories.

Fatima tried her very best to make Aisha think differently about Faisal. She used to try to organise dates for them both secretly and she would laugh and say they are only "meetings" because dates were not allowed. They were seen to be inappropriate as Aisha and Faisal were not married and people would talk. I asked Aisha if she was happy and if she liked Faisal enough to marry him. Her answer was "No" but there was nothing she could have done.

Aisha confronted Fatima before the engagement was decided and shared her feelings about the marriage to her, but Fatima's words were "He is perfect for you, he comes from a nice, respectable family, he is older than you so he will take care of you, you will not find anyone as nice as him." She went on to say "He is very shy and quiet; he does whatever he is told, so use that to your advantage. You can mould him just the way you want him to be and not like Kamran." Fatima was not prepared to listen to anything Aisha had to say.

Aisha said to Fatima "But I do not love him." Fatima was not shocked to hear this, her reply was "Love will come later; you will grow to love him." Aisha said "So do you love Kamran?" Fatima just ignored the question and Aisha asked her again, this time Fatima did answer and she said "Of course I do I have a daughter with him." But this was not a proper answer if she really did love him she would not hesitate to say yes. Fatima thought she knew best and she went on by saying "This is what mother and father would have wanted." She tried to make Aisha feel guilty by saying "This was mother's last wish, are you going to deny her that? Didn't mother mean anything to you?" Guilt in my family always played a large part as that was the only way Fatima or Yasmin knew they could get us to do what they wanted.

Fatima liked Faisal a lot and she was afraid that if Aisha did not marry him someone else would - well that was what she used to say but that was not completely true because Faisal and his family had high hopes of him coming to England. There were no other relatives for him to marry in England apart from Aisha and I. Aisha had no choice but to agree to the marriage, she could not do anything because we were both stuck in a country that we did not call home - there was no one we could have turned to. Fatima had our passports, we were afraid that we would have been forced to stay there if we disagreed with anything. Uncle Farooq and his family were very strict; he would have done anything to protect his dignity and reputation.

Aisha's engagement took place at Uncle Farooq's house, because it was a lot larger than Faisal's and Uncle Farooq felt it was his duty to have the engagement there because this is what our father would have done. Aunty Noreen came to the house with her family; they were all dressed up in their best clothes. Aunty Shaheen, Nazia and Bushra had prepared a feast for the occasion. There was brown rice with lamb, brown rice with chicken, samosas, pakoras and plenty of methai to celebrate.

Rings were exchanged between Aisha and Faisal after which Aisha was given her gifts and Faisal had his from Fatima. Aunty Noreen had to make a point to Aisha by saying "Faisal chose and brought all of your clothes himself, he put a lot of love and effort into picking them for you." Aisha just looked at me and smirked because she was not at all bothered even if he had flown to the other side of the world for them because he and the clothes meant nothing to her. Once the engagement had taken place Faisal and his family went home feeling very happy because the engagement was official and not just talk.

17 Experiencing life outside of the village

OUR STAY IN Pakistan was coming to an end. We had not done any travelling which I was not happy about because we had flown such a long way. Aisha and I were promised some sightseeing but no one was willing to keep their promise. Fatima was worried we did not have much time as Aisha's engagement preparations had taken up most of it. Fatima eventually gave in to Aisha and I and said we could go to Lahore.

Lahore is a city where Sameera, Kamran's sister, lived with her husband and their daughter Asma. Sameera had moved to Lahore a few years earlier when she married. Her husband was from Lahore and his family still lived there. Sameera had married into a wealthier family who were related from afar. Kamran had not seen his sister for many years and was really looking forward to seeing her and his niece.

I had heard so much about the city and how fantastic and modern it was compared to the village life that we were used to. Kamran's family would say "Lahore is like England, everyone dresses differently; it's a different world." Nazia was quick to say "There is a lot of freedom for girls there, which is not good." I had a fair idea why she would say that, but I could not be bothered to argue with her because no one apart from Aisha would understand me.

I knew Nazia was very restricted in what she could do or wear. None of the girls were allowed to work and most of the girls in the village were educated at home. Nazia also chose to cover herself in a burka which she wore every time she left the house. I could only watch in amazement as Nazia covered herself from head to toe even though it was absolutely boiling hot outside. Just looking at her made me feel faint. So I chose to ignore Nazia's comments as I liked the sound of Lahore and I could not wait to see for myself.

The trip was organised and Fatima, Kamran, Saba and Nazia were to join Aisha and I on the trip. I was not looking forward to Nazia coming along as she always nagged Aisha and I. She wanted us to be like the other girls, quiet and simple. We travelled by car for most of the journey accompanied by one of the local villagers who had a diving licence and a vehicle. The villager had agreed to take us to Lahore because he was going to visit relatives; he was more than willing to drive us as Kamran was a close friend of his.

The vehicle was not safe. No one was wearing a seat belt, the roads were bumpy and luckily they eventually evened out as we headed for the city. As we approached the city, the air smelt different; there was no "village smell". I could not smell animals or burning that I was used to smelling from the open fires that people in the villages used to cook their food on.

I felt a sense of freedom when I saw how different city life was from the village. I could see young girls and women walking on their own without a care in the world. The girls were out walking the streets on their own and there was no male acting as a bodyguard for them. I felt amazed by all of this; it was like I had never seen anything like this before. But I had in England I had just forgotten what it was like. Living in the village was very controlling and I felt trapped, it was unbearable.

I asked Fatima why the girls were walking out on their own, her answer to me was not very nice, she said "Their parents must not care enough for them; if they did, they would not let their daughter go out and flaunt herself." I replied "They are not flaunting themselves, walking out on your own is not wrong - it's just a bit of freedom." Kamran had overheard what I said and he was very angry; he said "These girls are not proper Muslims, look they are not even covering their heads." then he pointed at Nazia and said "This is what girls should dress like." Nazia was wearing a burka; you could only see her eyes. Aisha could see I was not going to win and that I knew I was better off staying quiet.

After a mile or two we arrived at Sameera's house. I remember thinking the house was not as spectacular as it was described back in the village. It was definitely different from the village houses. For a start there were no animals, there was no grass, no mud, no extra land. The staircase to the house was inside. There was an awful smell coming from the drains of the house and the houses nearby. I remember thinking the street outside was dirty and disgusting. I had thoughts of rats in my mind, it reminded me of when I was learning at school about the black plague and how the streets in London were infested with rats and dirt, there was dirt everywhere.

We were greeted by Sameera and her mother-in-law. We were then shown inside the house, it felt very stuffy. The house was like a terraced house but it felt half the size of an average one. I was expecting the inside of the house to have a modern feel because Kamran described it to be like the ones you would find in England. This was not the case; the inside of the house was a similar style to the village houses except there was a washing machine and a built-in kitchen. The kitchen was very basic and needed repairing.

Sameera offered us all cold drinks while we all sat down. But there was nothing for us to sit on, instead we all sat on the floor. Fatima found that strange as back in the village everyone sat on something. Tactfully, she said to me that sitting on the floor was good and that this is what Muslims should do. She went on saying "many, many years ago traditionally Muslims did sit and eat on the floor." I found this very uncomfortable as the floor was made of stone.

Sameera shared many stories with us about Lahore and how she enjoyed her life here. Later, we were joined by her husband Hassan. He had been working all day in the local town. We were all seated on the floor together that evening while Sameera served a meal that she had prepared. The meal was a very basic dish of boiled rice with Chicken curry. The meal was piping hot but there was no cutlery for us to eat with. I asked Sameera if she had a spare fork that I could use, she said no and that eating with your hands is better for you. "Allah will reward you she said." I tried my very best to eat with my hands but the food was too hot. I gave up because I was not prepared to burn my fingers any longer. I ate the food when it had cooled down.

Aisha was just as shocked as I was, she was expecting the house and surroundings to be really wonderful. We were under the impression that Sameera was well off since she married someone with money but we could see things were not as we hoped they would be. We were never told exactly what Hassan's profession was. Fatima was eager to find out and she constantly asked Kamran. But Kamran would not tell Fatima what she wanted to hear. She was sure that Kamran was hiding something from her and that Sameera and her husband were in financial trouble.

The whole trip to Lahore was beginning to be a disaster, we were not comfortable where we were staying. We felt like outsiders because Sameera would often hold whispered conversations with Kamran. The initial stay in Lahore was three days but we left a day earlier when Fatima fell out with Sameera because the children, Saba and Asma were not getting on.

18 Fatima shows her true colours

OUR STAY IN Lahore was very disappointing; we did not do any sightseeing. I really wanted to visit a mosque there which was highly recommended by uncle Farooq.

Back at the village we were asked by the rest of the family if we had enjoyed ourselves. By this point Fatima had had enough of everyone praising Sameera and saying how lovely her life and home was in Lahore - she was not willing to hear any more. She shouted at Aunty Shaheen and said "Your daughter is nothing but a beggar, she is not as grand as you make her out to be, her house is trashy, she cannot afford much, she hasn't even got basic cutlery." Aunty Shaheen was surprised at Fatima and she started crying. Kamran became very angry as he was very protective of his family, especially his mother and sisters; he was on the verge of hitting Fatima across her face but was stopped by his father, Uncle Farooq. He told Kamran to calm down and think about what he was about to do. Fatima was in uncontrollable tears and started praying for God to take her life because she felt like Kamran was an enemy to her, she felt all alone.

Then the argument started again. She wanted to know if the money that Kamran had been sending to Pakistan while he was in England was going to his sister and not to his parents and who it should have gone to. Kamran denied everything; he was adamant that his parents were the ones who received the money that he sent. Then Fatima wanted to know what they had spent the money on. Kamran could not answer her and he told his parents to stay quiet. By now the whole of the household were out in the yard watching and listening to this argument. Even the next door neighbours were lurking around the door wanting to know if everything was all right. The argument eventually fizzled out and Fatima and Kamran decided not to speak to each other.

As night fell we were all out in the yard again as it was very hot and the night was muggy and sticky. We were all sitting eating our food when Aunty Miriam, Uncle Ahmed's wife mentioned Faisal's name. She said to Aisha "Your fiancée has been asking about you while you were away." Aisha and I both knew this would happen as we got the impression that Aunty Noreen wanted her son Faisal to be married before Aisha left for England.

Fatima was sitting on a manji near us and overheard what Aunty Miriam had said. She became very angry and wanted to know why Faisal had been around to the house. She also wanted to know who else had come around while we were away in Lahore. Aunty Miriam gave in to Fatima as she was always the one to gossip and she could not keep a secret even if her life depended on it. She said Faisal and his parents came over to the house on a number of occasions to talk to Uncles Farooq and Ahmed. Fatima wanted know why. Aunty Miriam went on to say "They want Aisha and Faisal to be married before Aisha goes back to England." Fatima went shooting across to Uncle Farooq and she started to shout. She asked Uncle Farooq "What right do Faisal and his parents have asking you about the marriage?" She started talking to him like he was nothing.

Ever since I can remember Uncle Farooq was always seen as a father figure to us all. We used to call him "abba bader" which meant "older father", this stuck because he was older than our father and this was seen as a respectable name, we never referred to him as Farooq. But Fatima was really belittling him - none of his sons were prepared to stand by and watch Fatima insult him in such a way. So Nazia and Bushra had to drag Fatima away from Uncle Farooq. She was acting like a spoilt child.

Fatima felt like Uncle Farooq was making all the decisions, Fatima wanted to be in control of everything, she was the one who decided on Aisha getting engaged but she could not understand why everyone was asking Uncle Farooq.

Fatima eventually calmed down; Uncle Farooq explained what had happened. He said "Faisal's parents feel he is getting too old. Now that the engagement is official they want him to be married, they do not want to wait around." Fatima had said to Aunty Noreen that Aisha was only sixteen, she was going to go back to England to finish her studying in college and once that was done and at the age of eighteen she would come back to Pakistan and be married to Faisal.

Uncle Farooq listened to Fatima. He agreed with Fatima and felt that this was the right decision. Fatima and Uncle Farooq sat down and discussed Aisha and Faisal's situation. They both decided to speak with Aunty Noreen and Uncle Aqeel the following morning.

19   Fatima clears the air

THE FOLLOWING MORNING everybody was up early again. The sun was shining and it was beginning to get warmer by the minute. Fatima was busy getting dressed and ready, she wanted to see Aunty Noreen to clear the air and to get some facts straight with her. Fatima asked Aisha and I if we wanted to go along with her to see some distant cousins who lived in the same village. We said yes because we thought this would be a good way of meeting relatives who we were not familiar with. Imran joined us this time; he was acting as a bodyguard for us as the village was a very dangerous place for women.

We made half of the journey by horse and cart and we walked the remaining distance. As we walked up to the front of Aunty Noreen's house we were greeted by Aunty Shaheen's sister, Haleema who had seen us from the yard in her house next door. She was very happy to see us and she wanted to know why we had not been to see her. Fatima told her that we had been really busy and that our stay in Pakistan was coming to an end. She was very persistent with Fatima and literally begged her to see her before we went back home. Fatima did not like Aunty Haleema very much, we had heard a great deal about her, most of which was not good.

People said Aunty Haleema was a witch. As children if our parents thought we were naughty they would scare us by saying "Aunty Haleema is a witch, she will do black magic on you and she has ghosts that are very scary."

The years had not been very kind to Aunty Haleema. She was younger than Aunty Shaheen but she looked at lot older. Our mother used to say "She was very pretty once, but when she started doing black magic she became evil and it showed through her face." Aunty Haleema had a very dark complexion with big dark eyes. She had a sort of mystery about her. Our mother would say "If Aunty Haleema did not get what she wanted she would use black magic to get her way." Fatima and Yasmin had always been superstitious. Fatima blamed her arguments between Kamran and her on black magic. She would say to Kamran "It's your auntie's fault that we argue."

Fatima also blamed Aunty Haleema for her and Kamran not being able to conceive. They had been trying for children for a while; her daughter was not a baby any more, she was growing up fast and Fatima longed for another child. Kamran hated the fact that Fatima blamed anything bad that would happen on his aunty. Fatima even blamed Aunty Haleema for our Mother's cancer. She was sure that it was Haleema's doing and that she hated our family.

Fatima told Aunty Haleema that we had a very busy day ahead of us and that if we did have time we would stop for a drink. Aisha and I both knew this would not happen as Fatima would never drink anything from her house because she felt Aunty Haleema would spike our drinks. Aunty Haleema was very pleased and said to her "Make sure you do."

Fatima knocked on Aunty Noreen's door. Aisha and I were not sure if we should stay outside while Fatima spoke to Aunty Noreen. Imran assured us that nothing was going to happen and that it would be very rude if we did not go inside. Aisha was nervous because Faisal was sitting outside on a manji as we entered the door and into the yard. Faisal acted very shyly as Aisha walked past him - he kept his head down. I think he was told to act that way by his parents because they felt he had scared Aisha a little with his openness.

Aunty Noreen greeted us all with a kiss. She was a little surprised to see us as the village was a fair distance away. Aunty Noreen asked us what the visit was in aid of. Fatima did not tell her the real reason was to clear the air. Instead she said "Oh we came to see Aunty Gulab and her family and we were passing so we thought we would nip in and say hello." Aunty Noreen was happy and she offered us all something to drink. Fatima accepted, but said that we were only stopping for one.

While we were all sitting down and drinking our cold home-made lemonade, Fatima saw the opportunity to ask Aunty Noreen about what she had said to Uncle Farooq while we were away in Lahore. Aunty Noreen was quick in trying to explain that what she said was blown out of proportion. She went to on explain that her only intentions were to try to kill two birds with one stone. She thought since Aisha was already in Pakistan, it would be a good idea for her to get married while she was here. She went on to explain that it was a very logical idea, she said "I thought it would be easier for Faisal and Aisha to get married while Aisha is in Pakistan, as the plane tickets would be very expensive for her when she came back to Pakistan." she went on to say "We have brought lots of clothes for Aisha as gifts and I have seen a wedding dress for her." Fatima explained to her that Aisha was going back to England to college and once she had completed college she would travel back to Pakistan and would be married. Fatima went on to say "If you do not stop pressuring us, we will have to think again about the engagement." Aisha and I knew Fatima was only trying to scare her; she would never cancel the engagement as our mother wanted Aisha to marry her nephew and Fatima liked Faisal very much. Aunty Noreen apologised and said "I am sorry if this sounded too pushy for you, this was the last thing that I want to happen." She knew there was no other way for Faisal to go to England.

Once we had finished our drinks, we left for Aunty Gulab's, a few houses away.

20 Meeting more relatives

As WE WALKED to Aunty Gulab's house with Fatima and Imran at the front leading the way, I asked Aisha how she felt. Aisha said to me that she was glad that she was not getting married this time and that she hoped something would happen in the meantime or the next couple of years to break up the engagement.

The area that Aunty Gulab lived in was very dirty; there was a landfill site at the end of her house where local villagers dropped their rubbish. There was a lake next to it that was filled to the rim with dirt and rubbish and the smell was unbearable.

We were now a short distance away from the house and we were greeted by a herd of very poor looking children. Initially I thought they had come to us asking for food but Imran said they were not, they all lived in the house that we were going to. The children were just surprised to see us, they could tell we were new to the village and they were very excited. I was amazed, I could not believe so many children were living in that small house that I could see in front of me.

The entrance to her house was guarded with a large metal gate that creaked when it was opened. We were greeted by a young man who Fatima said was one of Aunty Gulab's sons but she was not sure which as she had about five in total. This son was called Amjad, he was very happy to see us. He welcomed us in and said "We were all waiting and wondering when you would come and see us."

As we entered the gate we were brought into the yard. The yard was not very large, not as large as uncle Farooq's or Aunty Noreen's and it was mostly occupied by manjis where people were sitting. As soon as we were seen, a rush of people made their way toward us. I had no idea who they all were. There were at least twenty of them if not more. Aisha and I could not believe that all these people were relatives. These relatives were never spoken of back in England, I did not know why but I was keen to find out.

One by one the women all hugged and kissed us and the men just touched our head with their hand to indicate embrace. Amongst the women there were four elder ones. One of whom I understood to be Aunty Gulab. All four of them began to cry as Fatima was being embraced by them all.

This was a regular thing that happened whenever we were met by people. They all seemed to do this with Fatima as they felt she knew what to do. They knew that Fatima was born in Pakistan and so she understood what the embrace was about. Aisha and I stood back and watched as our parents were mourned and their names were honoured.

After a while the four women turned towards Aisha and I. Amongst the four women were two elderly ones. The other two women introduced themselves. One was Aunty Gulab and the other was called Nargis, Aunty Gulab's younger sister.

Aunty Gulab looked as though she did not take very much care of herself and her appearance. When she spoke she had two very large front teeth that seemed to overlap immensely over her lower teeth as she spoke which made it hard for her to close her mouth. She was not very tall, about 5ft at a guess and she was of a round build. She too like all of the other women wore a salwar kameez with a head scarf to cover her head. Her clothes were not spectacular but very simple with little detail. She looked as though she had been cleaning all morning because her clothes were dirty. When she spoke she was very loud and she would laugh a lot in excitement. Her laugh was very funny to hear, she would chuckle to herself. Aisha and I found her to be very funny to look at as she reminded us of a beaver.

Her sister Nargis was quite the opposite, I think she was in her late twenties. She was slightly taller, of a slim build and her looks were not as bold and striking as her sisters. She came across very quiet and gently spoken.

The two elderly women were grandparents and great grandparents of some of the children who we saw earlier on. One of the women was Aunty Gulab's mother and the other was her mother-in-law. Both women came across to be very pleasant, they spoke very highly of our parents and family.

The whole house was full of people as we walked towards what looked like the kitchen. I noticed a few young men huddled up together in a corner. I asked Fatima who they were she told me that two of the men were Aunty Gulab's sons and the others were their cousins. Fatima was quick in telling me to stay away, I asked her why and she said "Mother and father did not get on with their parents; they were enemies for a long time." She said they had a dispute over some land that Aunty Gulab's husband had which was rightfully ours. She said this had happened a long time ago and that we are on speaking turns now but only just. I asked her "So why are we here today and visiting?" she said "Uncle Farooq wanted us to. One of the elder ladies is not very well and she is a close relation to our father and Uncle Farooq, she is their first cousin. She wants us to get on, it's like her last wish." I had no idea that this frail old lady that sat in the corner was our father's cousin.

21 Not another marriage proposal

AISHA AND I seemed to be the centre of attention once more. I was more so because I was still single. Aunty Gulab and her family congratulated Aisha on her engagement. They said to her that she was well suited to Faisal. Aunty Gulab went on to say how beautiful I was and she could not understand why I was not engaged. Fatima interrupted by saying "We do not have anyone suitable for her yet, maybe in a few years when we return, there will be someone for her, we do not want to rush into anything." I could sense Aunty Gulab's mind ticking, she was taking everything in. I knew what she was thinking and what was going to come next.

It was still the morning and we had been at Aunty Gulab's house for almost an hour. During this time I had noticed that like Uncle Farooq and Ahmed there were two families living under the one roof. Aunty Gulab was living in one part of the house with her family, her mother and her mother-in-law. Her family consisted of her husband Qasim with their sons Amjad, Ijaz, Omar, Rizwan and Salim. Amjad and Ijaz the elder two were married to their first cousins. Between them they had approximately six children. Omar had been promised to a cousin and was now engaged. Rizwan and Salim were not engaged. Rizwan was eighteen years old; he was not studying and did not have a job. Salim was the younger one; he was about thirteen and was going to a local school.

Aunty Gulab had two daughters too. The elder one Atiya was married with four children. She lived a few doors away and was at the house with her children while we were there. Their younger daughter Momina was about twenty two. I had heard from Fatima that her engagement had fallen through; she was engaged to a distant relative who was a lot wealthier than their family, in a different village.

In the second part of the house lived Nargis with her husband and their children. Nargis had quite a few younger children. I did not know very much about her family other than that she was married to her first cousin.

The house itself was very small. There were so many people and so little space. There was no bathroom in the house and I was desperate to go so Nargis took me to a nearby field which she said was safe for me to use. I had nothing to clean myself with apart from some grass which I pulled from the earth. I had not used the field as a toilet since the first time I had come to Pakistan when I was a little girl.

Since coming back to Pakistan I was under the impression that most things had improved and that village life was becoming more modernised. Uncle Farooq had a toilet and a shower. So coming here felt like I was taking some very large steps backwards. Within this short period I started to notice how poor Aunty Gulab and her family were. Just looking at the way everyone dressed compared to Uncle Farooq and Ahmed's family and the house itself made me think. I knew that Aunty Gulab had no immediate family in England, therefore she had no extra money coming in. Her husband worked at a local shop and was not earning a lot of money. I noticed that she was also being very generous and it made me think was she being extra nice to us for a reason?

A few moments earlier Aunty Gulab offered us all a drink. I noticed she did not have much in the house to give us because we were all sitting near to the tiny hut that was the kitchen.

She had called her son Salim over to her and she sent him somewhere. A couple of minutes later he came back to the house with some bottles of Fanta. He had been to the corner shop so those extra bottles of drink must have cost them a few rupees.

After we had sipped our drinks and were getting ready to leave she stopped us and said "Why don't you stay for some lunch?" It was nearly lunch time and she went on to say "You have a long journey ahead of you, by the time you get home you will have missed lunch." Imran was quick to say "No thank you, we must be on our way." He felt like we had outstayed our welcome. Fatima was then put on the spot as Aunty Gulab was very eager and said "We have prepared some food for you and look at your daughter she looks very hungry." So we stayed and had lunch.

Lunch was served in the yard and we all sat on a large rug. Aisha sat next to me with Nargis. The lunch consisted of white rice with lentils, This was a very cheap and easy dish to make. I could see why the dish was so simple because there were quite a lot of mouths to feed. Looking across the yard I could see at least thirty people that were eating. While we were all busy tucking into our lunch I noticed Rizwan looking in my direction. Fatima had noticed and she told me to pull my scarf over my head and to look down. I was feeling very awkward at this point. I was trying to eat my lunch when all I could see were two slightly unfocused eyes looking straight at me.

Rizwan took after his mother. His most distinctive features were his hair, smile and eyes. His hair was very curly and his eyes were very peculiar. One eye would look in a different direction to the other and his smile was very cheesy. He had a very wide grin. It reminded me of the film 'The Grinch'.

Aisha kept nudging me, she found it highly amusing. I was not amused as he was not my type at all. He was not attractive to me, he was taller than me but very thin. He was wearing a cream coloured salwar kameez with black rubber slippers. His arms were so thin that I could see the shape of his bones, it was hot he had his sleeves rolled up which was not flattering at all.

After ten minutes people started to move away from the rug after finishing their lunch. I waited for Aisha to finish because I did not want to get up on my own. So once Aisha had finished I moved away with her.

As Aisha and I walked towards a nearby manji to sit on, I was stopped by Aunty Gulab; she asked me what I thought about the food and hospitality. I said "I really enjoyed the food and company a lot." She went on to say "Have you noticed my younger son Rizwan? He is very handsome and he is around the same age as you." Aisha gave me a nudge. I was trying to keep a straight face but I found it hard with Aisha by my side. I could not give her an answer so I acted shy. She told me to have a think about it and she went on to say "He really likes you, he told me that when he first saw you, he knew you were the girl for him. He has fallen madly in love with you." I could not say a word, it was like I had completely frozen. Aisha could see from my reaction that I was shocked and uncomfortable. She took hold of my arm and we walked across towards Fatima. Fatima was already by the gate waiting to go. She was waiting for Saba to get back because she had gone to relive herself.

22   Am I engaged?

DURING THE JOURNEY back to the village I was completely silent - my mind was all over the place. I could not believe that Rizwan was in love with me. He had never spoken to me, not even a word. So how could he be in love with me? It was like a scene from a movie - *'Love at first sight'* sprung to mind. But that was in the movies, I certainly did not love him. I was living in the real world not a fantasy.

Back at the house, Bushra and Nazia asked us what we thought about Aunty Gulab's family. Fatima said they were very nice people but she could see they were very poor too. She said their house was falling to pieces and that there were so many people at the house. There were lots of children and she felt the house was used as a playground. Uncle Farooq asked Fatima how she felt we were treated. Fatima said to him "Aunty Gulab was very hospitable, she cooked us our lunch and she even sent her son to the corner shop to get us some drinks."

Aunties Shaheen and Miriam pulled me across to one side and said "What did you think of them?" But before I got a chance to reply to her question she went on to say "Did you manage to see their son Rizwan?" I was starting to realise that the whole trip was a plan all along. Fatima had taken Aisha and I but especially me to see Aunty Gulab and her family in the hope of me wanting to marry her son.

I was disgusted and something strange came over me. I

wanted to scream the house down, I felt like I was a bubbling kettle, that was left on the hob for too long and I was ready to explode. I stormed across to Fatima in front of everyone and said "You have no right, tricking me into seeing their family, who do you think you are? I hate Rizwan. I would never marry him!"

Fatima was just as shocked as I was; she had no idea that this was what was happening when her back was turned. She said to Uncle Farooq "This was your plan all along, you wanted us to go and see Aunty Gulab in the hope of Samina being persuaded by Aunty Gulab and her family." She went on to say "The quarrel was between our father, if he was still alive he would never have anything to do with that family, so why should things change now!" Uncle Farooq went on to say "Things have changed, we have sorted our differences out, they are a good family. Rizwan is a good boy, he is very obedient and has had a good upbringing by his parents." Fatima was very angry and went on to say "He has no education and does not have a job, not like Faisal, he is educated and is still wanting to learn more. Rizwan is just a drop-out - a nobody."

I had never seen Fatima like this before, defending my honour like this. I always thought Fatima favoured Aisha over me. She was always quick to attend to Aisha's needs and wants ever since we were little. All these years I felt like Fatima hated me. Fatima was in tears, Kamran was trying his best to console her but she was having none of it. She felt like he and his family had betrayed her.

That night, most of the household was silent. Aisha asked me how I felt. I was angry and upset. I did not love Rizwan and I felt like Fatima would change her mind and force me to get engaged to him.

Aisha was deeply saddened by the fact that people could stoop so low to take any opportunity to create heartbreak in other people's lives. I felt like it was just a game to them all.

Playing with our lives like that. They saw us as a prize at the end of a race. The prize was for whoever Fatima decided we were to marry.

I was just waiting in hope that when Fatima did calm down she would not change her mind and destroy my life as she did to Aisha forever.

The following morning Fatima was confronted by Uncle Farooq, he touched her head in embrace and said "You are like a daughter to me, I am sorry if I offended you yesterday." She was still a bit angry so she moved his hand across. He started to laugh and he said "You remind me of your father, he was like you, hot-headed and bad tempered." Fatima's expression changed as she too remembered how our father was. She took this as a compliment and said to Uncle Farooq "I am his daughter after all." With that they started to discuss the possible idea of Rizwan and I getting married. The discussion lasted quite a while with Aisha and I sitting on a manji alongside Nazia who was giggling.

I did not know where to look; my future was being decided right under my nose. They were all weighing the pros and cons of the marriage. The pros were that he was around my age, he came from a respectable family but most of all they felt if I were to marry him the two families would become a lot stronger.

The cons were that he was not educated, he could not speak English at all whereas Faisal could. If he came to England he would struggle to find a job. But Uncle Farooq went on to say "He can learn English here within the two years while Samina goes to college and when she returns there will be no communication barrier." I remember thinking that it will not change the fact that I am not attracted to him and we are two worlds apart. They seemed to have it all planned out apart from the most important part to me, which was *I did not love him, I had no feelings for him.*

After the discussion it was decided that I was to marry

Rizwan, even though I did not love him. Fatima's answer to me was "Don't worry, the love will come later once you get to know him." But was I going to fall in love with him? I did not want my life going the same way as my sisters.

That day, I was teased by all of the younger children in the house. They had learned that I was to be engaged and they kept teasing me about him which I was fed up with. As night fell, everyone was preparing for sleep. I could not sleep as the air was very humid, so most of the girls slept on the roof while the men kept watch there too. Kamran was there along with Imran. Kamran's manji was next to mine and Aisha's with Fatima on the opposite side.

I was looking up into the night sky as I could not sleep. The stars looked so magical and I wished I was somewhere else. Kamran noticed that I had been staring up into the sky for quite a while. He then said to me "I have noticed you have changed, you have become more distant."

"Distant, how?" I went on to say. He said "I can tell you are in love!"

"I am not in love," I said. "I just want to go home now. I have had enough here." I made up an excuse about it being time that we went home. He was having none of it and completely ignored me. I knew I was going to get nowhere here so I just turned onto my side and pretended to sleep.

The following day was our last in Pakistan. Fatima and the rest of the family were up early. Fatima said she needed to go out to do some last minute gift shopping, so she and Bushra went to the local market while Aisha and I stayed in.

That morning we had lots and lots of visitors, some were local villagers who came to say their goodbyes, some were relatives and amongst the relatives were Rizwan's parents and sister, Nargis. Uncle Farooq took Rizwan's parents into one of the rooms; he was going to tell them the so-called good news.

I could not bear it so I left and sat on the roof. I was followed by Nazia who wanted to know why I had gone upstairs on my own. I had just about had enough of everyone wanting to know what was up with me when they knew I was not happy with the engagement.

Nazia was on the receiving end of my anger once more. She said that I was being silly and that Rizwan and I were made for each other, we were well suited. She could not understand my point of view. She kept saying "You are so lucky, you have someone who loves you.", "Loves me?" I said, "He does not love me, the only thing he loves is my passport." With that Nazia, gave me a very ashamed look and said, "You do not know what it is like being with someone that does not love you, that hits you, that cannot bear to be in the same room as you." I could see that she was talking from experience and that she was referring to her own relationship. But this was not the same thing I thought. To be loved means everything, but she could not see that, she felt like I was being ungrateful, that I did not love him back and with that I ran down the steps towards Aisha.

When I got to the Yard, I saw Rizwan's mum, Aunty Gulab, eating methai with Aunties Shaheen and Miriam - they were celebrating my engagement to Rizwan!

Nearby, I saw his father Rahim and Uncles Farooq and Ahmed also eating methai and they were joined in a toast, celebrating the two families coming together. I was called over by Aunty Gulab who then kissed me several times and she welcomed me to her family.

Shackled to my Family

23 Going back home at last

THAT EVENING, AUNTY Gulab and her husband Rahim stayed for several hours at the house. Soon after, they were joined by the rest of their family. Faisal and his family were also at the house that evening. They had come to realise that I was engaged to Rizwan and they did not seem to want to give me their blessing. I felt like Aunty Noreen was keeping her distance from me. She was very cold towards me, but I was not bothered; she was just another greedy person who wanted her son to go to England.

Rizwan's family stayed for quite some time at the house, all they seemed to do was to talk about me to the rest of Kamran's family. Aunty Gulab kept saying to Aunty Miriam how lucky she was to have such a beautiful daughter-in-law. I was sitting by Nazia and Bushra - they kept looking at me and smiling. Fatima and Aisha were indoors doing their packing.

Aunty Gulab was eager to know what my plans were when I got back to England. I said would be taking further education at college. She was very happy and she then said to me "Oh yes, and when you complete your education you will come back here and marry Rizwan. While you are away Rizwan will be learning English too." It seemed to me that she did not really care about what I said; all she was bothered about was the marriage. I really did not care if Rizwan learned English - it was not going to change the fact that I detested him and could not bear the thought of ever marrying him.

While everyone was having a good time celebrating my engagement, I noticed Rizwan was lurking around. He looked as though he really wanted to talk to me. He was waiting for an opportunity to come over to me. While this was going on I moved across to a different manji to where Aisha was sitting and we were talking about how exciting it was finally being able to go back home. Eventually Rizwan came over and said in Urdu "How are you?" These were the first words he had ever spoken to me. He looked nervous and he had something in his hands that he was playing with. He kept his head lowered. I said to him "I am fine, thank you." He went on to say "Have you enjoyed your time in Pakistan?" I said "It was ok." Then Fatima came over to us, she had a smile on her face. With that, I made an excuse of "I have forgotten to pack something, I am just going to get it." So I quickly went into a nearby room where most of my things were. I was joined by Rizwan a few moments later, he stopped me packing and took hold of my hand and he said in Urdu "Do not forget me when you are in England, I love you." I quickly pulled back my hand and said in English "Go away!" I got the impression he did not understand what 'go away' meant because he did not move an inch. So instead I moved away and walked back to the yard.

It was soon time for everyone to leave as it was very late and we were due to fly back to England in a few hours. Aunty Gulab was very emotional as she hugged and kissed every one of us. I was dreading my turn so I walked away pretending that I was thirsty and needed a drink. Aunty Gulab had seen that I was walking away and she quickly rushed towards me and hugged me very tight. She called me her daughter and said "Do not be a stranger, when you go back home, make sure you keep in touch with us and write and make regular phone calls." I said I would, just to keep her happy. She hugged me once more and then she walked back to the rest of her family. I was hugged by the rest of her family too, her daughters and grandchildren. Her grandchildren called me Aunty and her daughters and sons called me sister-in-law. They already had it in their minds that I was their sister-in-law.

Faisal and his family had left an hour earlier and now it was Rizwan and his family's turn to say their goodbyes. Everyone made their way to the entrance of the house. Apart from me, I pretended I had a headache and I was sitting alone by the kitchen when Rizwan came over and handed me a letter. He told me to read it in private. I had a fair idea about what was going to be written in the letter and with that he left.

I opened the letter, it was written in English. I knew it was not Rizwan who had written the letter as he could not read or write English. He must have had someone else write it for him. The letter was a love letter, there were red hearts in it and in every corner of the letter read "I love you!" I had never been given one of these before. But this letter looked very familiar to me, I had seen these sorts of letters before when Shazia, Yasmin and Fatima got married. They too had these letters from their husbands. In this letter it said how much Rizwan had fallen head over heels in love with me. I found this very cheesy and I felt disgusted inside. So I went into the kitchen and threw it across the open fire.

Soon after, Aisha came over and asked me what Rizwan was doing in the kitchen with me. I told her and she laughed and said "Have you kept the letter? You should. Keep it under your pillow and look at it before you sleep." She could see that I was not sharing this joke with her so she stopped and said "I am sorry, I could not help it, you can't help but laugh, right?" It's so sad how these people think just by writing a love letter that your feelings would change towards them.

I asked Aisha if she had been given any such letters from Faisal, she said no but he did give her his number and a photograph of himself. This time it was my turn to tease her and I said "Was it taken fifteen years ago?" She did not find this joke amusing, but I did as he was a lot older than her and it seemed to be the appropriate joke at the time. She said "he wants me to call him when I get to England and every week without fail. I asked him if he had a mobile phone and he said no, he would be using a mobile from his next door neighbour." She then went on to say "I will not be calling him, I have lost his number.", "That's very convenient." I said.

The night had been so long and it was time for us to travel to the airport. We had not slept and I was very tired. Saying goodbye to Uncle Farooq and Uncle Ahmed and his family was very hard as I had grown attached to them. All in all they had been very kind to us and I was going to miss Uncle Farooq's stories of his childhood growing up with our father and his army stories, but nonetheless I was glad I was going home. Everyone was very emotional, Aunty Shaheen was trying to hold her tears back by saying "This is not goodbye, we will all meet again in a couple of years and have two very big celebrations." With that everyone agreed.

Imran and Uncle Farooq took us to the airport with the help of his friend again who had driven us to the village when we first arrived. I was sad to leave but very happy at the same time.

24 Moving On

ON THE PLANE back home I relaxed as I tried to clear my mind from all the thoughts I had about Pakistan. I wanted to move on and try my very best to enjoy the next two years that I called 'freedom'. I was going to enjoy that time by trying to be myself. But what was being myself going to be like? Had I been myself before? I had forgotten what it was like.

After a lengthy eight hours we landed at the airport and collected our luggage. We were met by Kamran's friend who was a taxi driver and was going to drive us back home. On the journey he asked us all how our holiday in Pakistan went. Kamran said it was great, we wanted to stay longer but the girls, (he was referring to us) are starting college so we had to cut the holiday short. I remember thinking the so-called holiday was six weeks long. This was not short especially when we did not do much sightseeing and spent the majority of our time indoors. The taxi driver then went on to say, "Did you do anything out of the ordinary while you were there?" *Out of the ordinary* I thought, then it hit me, was it everyone's plan all along for Aisha and I to get engaged? I had my suspicions about the trip from the very beginning; there were too many co-incidences. Kamran's reply was "Yes, we have some good news, Aisha and Samina, my sister-in-laws are engaged." The taxi driver was overwhelmed and congratulated Kamran and Fatima. Aisha and I kept quiet.

The taxi driver then said, "Are the future grooms related?" Kamran's reply was "Yes but I am gutted that I do not have any younger brothers for the girls to marry. It would have been fantastic if we could have kept the relation closer in the family." I could not believe what I was hearing. There were already two of our sisters married to two brothers and Shazia's marriage was not far off making it three as Kabir was my Uncle Ahmed' son.

The subject was soon changed as Fatima felt Kamran was trying to take all of the credit from her. She was the one who was acting as a mother, a parent to us. She gave Kamran the look that he was used to seeing, which basically meant 'keep quiet, or else.'

Aisha and I were exhausted; Saba was asleep, she had been asleep for most of the journey. As we pulled up to the front of the house I noticed the curtains twitching in the front room. It was Abdul, our brother, he had been eagerly waiting for our arrival. As soon as we pulled up to the front of the house, the entrance door was opened and out came Yasmin, Abdul, Hamid, Laila and Nadia. They all welcomed us and carried our bags inside. Arriving home seemed surreal. Odd in some respects but that did not last for long. Yasmin got straight to the point and said "Congratulations" to Aisha and I, Abdul just laughed and said "I told you both that you will get married before I do."

Before we went to Pakistan we were constantly getting phone calls and letters from relatives wanting our hand in marriage and from then on Abdul would argue and tease Aisha and I by saying he will never get married to someone in Pakistan and if he did he would make sure that Aisha and I were married before he was.

Abdul was very spoilt, he had a sort of 'I told you so' expression on his face. He felt like he had won the so-called bet. But the victory was short lived; I reminded him that I was not technically engaged. There was no engagement ceremony for me. Aisha was engaged officially, mine was just on Fatima's and Uncle Farooq's word.

Yasmin had overheard this argument that Abdul and I were having. She asked Fatima why an official engagement had not taken place. Fatima said to her that we had run out of time and that the engagement was a last minute thing.

I was stunned to hear that Yasmin had never met Rizwan or his family before. She asked Fatima why the engagement took place. Fatima Said "I did call to tell you what was going on and you said to go ahead because you felt it was the right thing to do under the circumstances." The circumstances were that Aisha and I were going to college and that college was seen to be somewhere Muslim girls especially us could dishonour the family name by having relationships with the opposite sex. Fatima felt that getting Aisha and I engaged was the only way to stop people from talking and they knew how much we wanted to learn and further our education.

Aisha and I were the key topic for quite some time, it was nearly mid-afternoon and we were jet-lagged. Yasmin was dying to know what presents we had brought back for her. She knew that Imran was going to send her some because she was very much in love with him and she called and wrote to him on a regular basis. Imran had sent Yasmin lots of gifts. In Pakistan, Fatima was very angry with Imran because he was filling up all of her suitcases with presents for Yasmin. I noticed a touch of jealously from Fatima towards Yasmin, Imran seemed to be very different to Kamran. He seemed to appreciate Yasmin more than Kamran appreciated Fatima. I felt Imran did not take his relationship for granted. But the thought did cross my mind if Imran's generosity was all for show and that this was all part of his plan to live in England.

So Fatima started to open up the suitcase and I was right, most of the gifts were for Yasmin. I had not seen what Fatima had packed. Inside her suitcases were clothes for Laila, Shazia and Nadia from Aunty Miriam and Aunty Shaheen. There were also *banga* in the suitcases, these were traditional Indian bangles. Nazia and Bushra had sent these for Laila and Nadia. Shazia had a few items from her mother-in-law Miriam but not many as Aunty Miriam was always moaning about how poor she was and she could not afford to buy any luxuries.

Before left for Pakistan Shazia had given Fatima an envelope with some money inside for Aunty Miriam. But looking at the clothes that Aunty Miriam had brought for Shazia, you could see the money was not spent on them. Fatima had a couple of other suitcases that contained gifts for Uzma, Sophia and Sophia's daughter Salma. These gifts were from Aunty Noreen and her family. Imran had also brought gifts for Salma his daughter which Yasmin was not happy about.

After a while I became bored of looking at all of the gifts and listening to Yasmin and Fatima talking about our relatives back in Pakistan. There was a lot of bitchiness going on in their conversation. Fatima told Yasmin about how Aunty Shaheen treated her daughter Nazia like a princess and how for most of the time Saba, her daughter was pushed aside by Kamran's family. This was not entirely true. Fatima always wanted to feel like she was the centre of everyone's attention and when someone else was in the limelight she did not like it. The majority of Kamran's family knew what Fatima was like but chose to keep quiet. There were a few arguments between Fatima and Nasreen. Nasreen had four children who were very naughty, they would pick on Saba and Fatima would then argue with Nasreen.

Aisha and I decided to walk away and make our way up to our bedroom. This was our first chance to speak openly about what we had been through. Aisha, like me was not happy with our engagements and the thought of having our future decided for us. We were looking forward to a fresh start at college. We knew that making friends was going to be hard as the college that we were going to was chosen by Fatima and Yasmin and our school friends would not be studying there. The start of college was approaching fast and Aisha and I decided not to say a word about our engagements to anyone.

Shackled to my Family

25 First day of college

WE HAD ONLY days before Aisha and I were due to start college. Preparing for college was easy as we had most of our clothes and stationary already. Fatima and Yasmin would not allow Aisha and I to wear any western, non-Pakistani clothing. Kabir, Shazia's husband was a preacher in the making and took pride in getting the message of Islam across. One of his key principals was that Muslim women should dress like Muslim women. Shazia would always cover her head with a scarf and she was always seen in Pakistani dress.

The college was roughly a mile away from Shazia and Kabir's house. He knew that we were going to college and he was not happy about it. He said to Kamran on many occasions that "Aisha and Samina should have got married before they start college." In his mind he was convinced that we would disgrace the family and in turn his reputation as an upstanding pillar of the community.

The day came for Aisha and I to enrol in our chosen course. I found this nerve-racking; I had butterflies in my stomach while Aisha and I walked to the college.

Aisha and I had not interacted with the opposite sex since primary school and for the last five years we were studying at an all-girls school. As we walked, Aisha said to me how nervous she was but excited at the same time. She said the excitement was more overpowering than the nervousness and that we would soon be fine once we got into the swing of things.

Aisha and I decided to enrol on the same course as we both enjoyed computers and had similar interests. As we entered what seemed to be a meeting, we were approached by an enrolment officer who asked us if we had signed up for two year course. She then went over to a few other people who were in the same situation as us.

During this time, the room began to fill up and soon after, our teacher Henry arrived. He welcomed us all, told us about the course and what it entailed. He then led us all into a computer room which he said was where most of our lessons would be taking place.

After Henry had handed out documents for the course he spent a couple of hours explaining the criteria and requirements of each section of the college syllabus. After which it was lunch time and we were told we could have a break.

This break gave Aisha and I the opportunity to meet and talk to other people in our class. We had seen a few Pakistani girls at the start of the class - they were sitting together and looked as though they had known each other for a while. Aisha and I went to say hello, I was very nervous about approaching people that I did not know but Aisha assured me that if we did not do this we would never be able to open up and be ourselves. So Aisha made the first move and introduced us. The ice-breaker was for the girls to ask us if we were twins. This was a good start as it lead to many questions such as what school did you go to and what made you choose this course. In return we were able to ask the girls questions.

We all made our way to the canteen where there were lots of Pakistani students. Entering the canteen was nerve-racking. There were people sitting on either side of the room and as you walked through it was like a catwalk where all the eyes were on you. Aisha and I got plenty of looks from the Pakistani students, especially the girls. I could see Aisha felt just as awkward as me. As we walked, I found myself lower my gaze and I fixed my eyes to the floor. I was very nervous; I could not understand why I was feeling so afraid, maybe it was the new surroundings and seeing so many people was beginning to be too much for me. I could not see Aisha's reaction, I was too busy thinking about what I was doing and I felt like I was going to trip up and embarrass myself.

We made our way to the food stand where I asked our new friend Farida why people had the tendency to stare. She said it was because we were twins. Maybe people around here have not seen many twins and the fact that we are both pretty and Pakistani and new to the college. I found Farida to be a very sweet person.

There were four girls in total, Javeria, Farida, Tabassum and Raheela. Javeria and Raheela were the eldest ones - they were two years older than us and had studied first at the college a couple of years earlier. Tabassum and Farida were a year older than us. I had seen Tabassum before and she recognised Aisha and I. She had gone to the same secondary school as us. All four girls lived in the same area as our sister Shazia and her family. We got to learn that Farida lived around the corner from Shazia and Tabassum knew Kabir from her Father. Kabir went to the same mosque as her father and paid regular visits to his house. Kabir was keen on digital TV and he used to try to get the latest Asian channels available for himself and Tabassum's father.

After we had finished our lunch it was time for us to return to our lesson. By then, the canteen was virtually empty and I was not worried about tripping up and making a fool of myself walking on that dreadful catwalk.

As we entered the computer room, Tabassum asked Aisha and I if we wanted to sit with them, so we did.

Soon our first lesson was over and the girls asked us if we wanted to stay for a bit and grab a snack or something. Aisha and I wanted to but it was nearly time for us to go home and if we did not go home on time especially on our first day Fatima and Yasmin would accuse us of all sorts of things as they already did not trust us. So Aisha and I made up an excuse of "We have relatives coming around tonight and we really need to start preparing the evening meal." This was a complete lie. as we never had any relatives who came to our home.

26 Life after college hours

THAT EVENING WE returned home feeling very happy. Yasmin asked Aisha and I what we had done at college that day. We told her that we enrolled onto a computer course and that we had made some friends on the course. Yasmin wanted to know who these friends were; she wanted to know if they were male or female. She only asked about them, she was not interested in what we were studying. She wanted to know who their parents were and where they lived. Aisha and I chose not to tell Yasmin much about our new friends that we had made. We knew that both Yasmin and Fatima would only say horrible things about them if the situation occurred when they were accusing us of something. We said that the friends were all girls, that they lived close to the college and that one of them used to go to the same school as us. Yasmin chose not to believe, she was adamant that these friends were male. I tried my very best to tell her otherwise but it fell upon deaf ears. With that Aisha and I took our belongings and headed for our bedroom.

While we were upstairs, Aisha and I talked about our first day at college. We were very happy about the time we spent there and coming home just threw all of the happiness out of the window. I said to Aisha "Why does Yasmin have such a shallow mind, why does she always have to accuse us of things that we have not done." I asked Aisha these questions but I knew the answers to them myself. I thought by asking someone else this may help me come to terms with the thoughts that I was having. I wanted Aisha to prove me wrong but she too knew that Yasmin was bitter and twisted. She wanted to control us like our parents controlled her.

A couple of hours later, Yasmin called for us from the bottom of the stairs; she had prepared some vegetable curry for our evening meal and wanted Aisha and I to do the cleaning and washing up. So I devised a rota where one week I was to do the cleaning and the washing up and Aisha would do the following week. Aisha felt this was not fair as Yasmin was not working and she spent most of her time at home. Aisha and I were also helping out with the cooking. Aisha wanted Yasmin to be a part of the rota so she included her in the rota. But when Aisha went downstairs to talk to Yasmin about the rota she became extremely angry. She did not want to be included, she wanted Aisha and I do all of the cleaning and the washing up.

Both Aisha and I built up courage and said "We are not going to do any of the cleaning or washing if you are not on this rota." While we confronted Yasmin the phone began to ring, it was Fatima. She would call like clockwork every evening. Yasmin answered the call and told Fatima what was going on. Fatima took Yasmin aside and said to her that we were very spoilt and this freedom that we were given was turning out to be a mistake. Yasmin in return agreed with everything. You could tell in her voice that she wanted to hit us.

I assured Aisha that being confrontational was the best way because Yasmin was used to getting her own way and she wanted to control us. She was treating us like slaves. Yasmin was in a rage, she slammed the phone down after speaking to Fatima.

Fatima was making the situation worse by adding fuel to the fire. Yasmin grabbed Aisha and slapped her a few times and I quickly went to her aid because I could not stand by and watch her being abused in such a way. As I did, Yasmin went to hit me - she was holding a stick in her hand. The stick struck my left arm. I was in agony; I thought Yasmin had broken my arm because I was in so much pain. Everyone else in the family just watched as Yasmin went for another hit. She thought by hitting us we would listen to her and she would get what she wanted.

Abdul was sat on the kitchen chair watching and he was egging Yasmin to put more force into it. He was sitting back, enjoying the view. Hamid wanted to help us but he was told by Abdul to stay away as he had nothing to do with it. Hamid was on our side, he hated Abdul because he was very much like Fatima and Yasmin. He had the same views as them. Hamid was different; even though he was a lot younger than us he could see that Aisha and I were very badly treated.

By now I had taken quite a few hits from Yasmin and I could not bear any more. I was beginning to see red and I was ready to fight back. I wanted to return some of the pain to Yasmin that she had done to Aisha and I. So I went for the nearest thing I could see which was a spare kitchen chair. I threw the chair at Yasmin which hit her on her back. The chair fell to the floor with one of its legs broken. My own strength startled me and once I had thrown the chair and hit Yasmin, I began to quiver. I was not sure what her reaction was going to be.

Yasmin screamed in agony, she had not expected this from me. She started to cry and cursed the day I was born. All this time I kept saying to her, "You cannot hit me any more, I will not allow you to control me like this. Who do you think you are? You are nothing to me." Aisha told me to calm down and said "She is not worth it, this is what her life is about." I was crying at this point because she had hit a nerve inside of me which triggered the tears, but why are we always bullied by them? I also meant Fatima as she too tried her very best to bully us.

Aisha and I saw our chance to leave quickly for our bedroom where we were able to lock the door before Yasmin could attack me again. Aisha and I quickly ran up the stairs and into our bedroom. Moments later there was a banging sound coming from the door - it was Yasmin. She demanded that we open the door as she wanted her revenge. Aisha and I were afraid, we had been on the receiving end of Yasmin's punishments before but this time was different because we had never laid a finger on her. She was not going to leave. I thought she was going to break the door down because it was beginning to shudder. Aisha and I had nowhere to go, we were trapped.

The bedroom was on the second floor and the thought did cross my mind of jumping out of the window. We had no telephone in our bedroom or a mobile phone as we were not allowed one so we could not call for help. Eventually, after endless attempts by Yasmin to break the door down she gave up and went downstairs. Aisha and I sat on the floor motionless, we hated ourselves.

Aisha and I had spent the best part of an hour locked up in the bedroom when there was a knock on the door. Aisha asked who it was and what they wanted. It was Laila and Nadia, they wanted to come in as it was very late and they had school in the morning. Our sisters shared the same room as us. They had bunk beds, Laila Slept on the top and Nadia at the bottom. Both Aisha and I had single beds. The room that we were sleeping in was our parents' room when they were alive. This room was passed over to us because there were not enough rooms in the house for us all. So all of the remaining girls had to share the largest room in the house. The boys Abdul and Hamid slept in one of the upstairs rooms that was once Fatima and Kamran's. It was Yasmin's intention from the very start to have Laila and Nadia in the same room as us because she thought this was a good way of her keeping an eye on us - Laila was very nosey; she would always watch Aisha and I and she would then tell Yasmin what she found out.

27 New found friendships

THE NEXT FEW months were some of the best. Aisha and I were loving college and our new-found friendships. We were getting on like a house on fire with all four girls. I had grown to notice a great many things about these girls.

Raheela was always the quiet one; she dressed in traditional Pakistani clothing. She never wore a headscarf on her head but she did have one around her neck. She occasionally wore the western style of clothing but she always had a long cardigan on to cover her shape. Raheela was a medium build, she was slightly taller than me, had medium length dark hair and she always wore glasses. She never wore any make-up and she said she never needed to as her complexion was fine the way it was.

I could see that Raheela was very clever. She always seemed to get stuck-in whenever we had a lesson. She would find a great sense of achievement when she got the grades she aimed for - she was always very focused. Javeria would say "Raheela can achieve the grades she wants because she has no worries, she does not have to help out at home, she is treated like a princess." I found this remark unfair as Raheela was always such a hard worker.

I had learned that Raheela was the only girl in her family and that her parents always wanted the best for her. She would tell me that her mother never allowed her to do any of the household chores. She was always told by her parents that once she had finished her evening meal which her mother always prepared to go up to her study room and start her college work. I never even knew what a study room was until Raheela told me. She said she had most of the equipment that a study room needed in there such a computer, a desk and bookcase. Raheela was most friendly with Farida and Javeria because they had gone to the same school together. Farida would always speak very highly of Raheela and her family.

In our family we had the one computer which was always in Yasmin's room. She had bought this computer with her hard earned cash when she was studying at university. The computer was Yasmin's pride and joy and she hated anyone else using it.

Javeria was quite the opposite of Raheela but nevertheless they got on very well. She was very loud and she always spoke to the opposite sex. She had bags of confidence whereas Aisha and I had none. Javeria mostly wore western clothing. I really liked her dress sense, she always looked smart and she seemed to carry herself well. Like Raheela, she was the only girl in her family. She had two younger brothers who she loved very much - she always talked about them. Javeria had black, shoulder length hair which was always straight and looked nice. She would get her hair styled and cut on a regular basis. She always wore make-up and I also noticed that Javeria had a new mobile phone almost every month. This lead me to believe that her parents must have been very well off.

Farida was the most different of the rest of the girls. She wore a head scarf and Pakistani clothing. She never wore western clothing because like my family, hers was very strict. She spoke in a very soft voice. She was very thin and tall. Farida was not the only girl in her family; she had an elder sister who had children and a couple of elder brothers too. Farida had a handful of nieces and nephews who she always talked about. She always seemed to talk more about her older niece than anything. Farida told me her older niece was about fourteen years old but going on twenty. She said that her niece would get away with murder and that she was very spoilt by her parents.

Finally, Tabassum like Farida always wore a headscarf, she was very pretty. She was slightly more voluptuous than the other girls and was taller. Tabassum was the only child in her family. She resembled a girl that I used to know back at secondary school. I later found out that this girl was Tabassum's cousin. Tabassum had very beautiful eyes, she had a bubbly personality and she always spoke her mind. I found her to be very funny too.

Aisha and I were becoming very fond of these girls. I got on really well with Javeria and Tabassum and I looked up to them even though they were only a few years older. They always seemed to be very pleasant and their personalities always shone. Tabassum was very kind; she would always tell me how pretty I was. I did not believe her, I hated myself and believed myself to be very ugly. Tabassum would say "Look over there, that guy is checking you out." and I was so shy that I never looked.

It was winter, and the month of Ramadan. All of our friends were fasting and most of the college was too - the vast majority were Muslim as the college was situated in an area with a large Pakistani community. In this month, my friends and I used to sit together at lunch time. Whenever we had a free period, we would catch up on Bollywood movie gossip and generally have a laugh. I was starting to come out of my shell.

During this time we had a new girl who started our class - she was Pakistani too. She started the course late as she had studied her first couple of months at a different college but she chose to leave there because and she was not enjoying it. Her name was Hajira - she was the same age as Aisha and I. She was from a different town and she commuted to college every morning. Most of the time she was late because she travelled to the college by coach. It was a standing joke in our class by our tutor, Henry, that whenever there was a knock on the door it was always Hajira.

She was always very funny when she made her entrance, she would be huffing and puffing as she got to her chair and she would always slam her bag down and then share the ins and outs of her journey.

Hajira was very slim, she was not as pretty as Tabassum but she did turn some heads as she was very tall and had a figure to die for. She mainly wore western clothing. She always wore a headscarf as well; her mother was strict and her elder sister was married to a religious man who she found very intimidating. Her father had passed away a few years earlier and her mother was always very protective of her and, like my mother, she did not want Hajira to disgrace her family.

Hajira and I became very close; she had the same interests as me. She loved fashion and make-up. Hajira was never allowed to wear any make-up as her mother hated it. So she would leave the house with none on and once she went on the coach she would do her make-up there or she would put it on in college.

28 Watching and learning

HAJIRA WAS GETTING a lot of attention from the boys at college. She would say that she did not like the attention but secretly I could tell she loved every minute of it.

Beside Hajira, I was starting to feel very uncomfortable; she was always seen as being very attractive by most of the boys. Whenever we would go to the canteen at lunch times Hajira would always make sure she walked ahead of us all and made an entrance. She would always get stares from all the boys there. This would make the rest of us nervous and anxious about ourselves. Hajira would steal all of the limelight.

I felt, compared to me, that she was very beautiful but Javeria assured me that she wasn't and that the only reason why she was getting all of the attention was because she carried herself well and she came across to be very confident. Hajira always wore tight clothing. Her jeans always showed off her skinny frame. I wanted to be like her, I wanted to dress in western clothing but I was too afraid of what might happen to me if I did. I knew Kamran and Kabir would disapprove and then they would blame the college that I went to for leading me astray.

Hajira came from a very large family, there were no boys but she was one of eight girls. Her father had passed away when she was very young and the only person who she said she had to answer to in her family was her mother. She talked about her elder sister a lot and said she was a practising Muslim who always covered up and prayed five times a day. Her other sisters were the complete opposite.

Hajira always praised her family and said her sisters were very beautiful. I got the impression she thought she was a better class than the rest of the girls at college. I was seeing a different side to her, a bitchy and vindictive side. I felt all of the attention that she was getting was going to her head.

Hajira always seemed to have a new piece of clothing on every week. I used to wonder how Hajira managed to afford all of the nice clothes that she was wearing. I used to be very inquisitive when I noticed anything new that she was wearing. She would tell me that all of her sisters were roughly the same build and that they borrowed each other's clothing.

I wanted to wear western clothing too but Aisha and I did not have much money. The only money that we did have was the EMA that we received from the government for attending college. So in the next few weeks Aisha and I were very strict about what we spent our money on. We managed to save a small amount and treated ourselves to a shopping trip to buy some western clothing.

Aisha and I devised a plan and we chose not to tell Yasmin about any free periods that we had. So if we were not at college we were in town. But we always made sure the day before we found out exactly what Yasmin and Fatima were to doing just to be sure we never got caught.

Aisha and I knew Yasmin and Fatima would be very angry when they found out what we were up to but this was our only way of doing something that we wanted. Because our life was very boring, the only thing that we seemed to enjoy was going to college. We were getting our work done and also having a bit of fun at the same time.

Aisha and I were fed up of living by the rules of our family. We were young adults now, we were not children any more. So one day when we had a free period Aisha and I along with

Javeria and the rest of the girls went to our local town and did some shopping.

Javeria had a great eye for clothing. I had been watching what the other girls were wearing at college and I knew exactly what I wanted. I was not going to go wild and buy a skirt or something because I knew skirts were forbidden in my family even if they were long. Our mother hated them even though in most of the Muslim countries women wore long skirts and not trousers. My mother hated trousers too as she thought it showed off the shape of a women's bottom.

After a couple of hours shopping Aisha and I had bought four items of clothing each. Two tops, one pair of trousers and a pair of jeans. I loved trying on clothes, initially I did not know what size I was so I had to take a few sizes with me to the changing room; in the end I discovered I was a size 12.

Javeria and the girls found the clothes to be very flattering on me. They said I had such a nice figure and that I looked like a completely different person. Aisha had brought similar clothes to me but we decided while choosing the clothing that we would buy different colours so we could borrow each other's as we were the same size.

Aisha and I went home that evening feeling afraid and nervous about what Yasmin would say. We made sure when buying the clothing that none of them were revealing because this was the last thing that we wanted. Once Aisha and I got to the house we sneaked in the back door where we would not get noticed because we did not have a key to the front door. Yasmin thought if Aisha and I did have a key this would be too much freedom for us to enter and leave the house whenever we wanted to. Before we entered the back door, Aisha hid the bags behind a broken fence that was resting against the wall in the garden. We both walked into our kitchen and we saw that no one was there so we quickly grabbed the bags making sure we did not make a sound and ran up the stairs to our bedroom.

Aisha was afraid of what Yasmin would do when she found out as she would blame college and our friends for influencing us.

Abdul had seen us sneaking upstairs so he followed us. He had seen the bags and he was always there when we never wanted him to be. Yasmin had not seen us as she was in the next room. Abdul followed us up the stairs shouting at the top of his voice. "Where have you been and what is inside those bags?" He wanted us to get into trouble. Aisha and I were not quick enough for him. He managed to get inside the room before we could lock it.

I made Abdul promise not to say anything to Yasmin if I told him where we had been and what was inside the bags. I was a fool for believing him because as soon as I told him he went downstairs to tell Yasmin. Aisha warned me not to tell him because she knew he could not be trusted. I knew she was right deep down but a part of me wanted her to find out because there was no way we were going to get away with wearing the clothes to college without her seeing us. Moments later, I heard her coming up the stairs and towards our room. I knew it was her because she always walked stamping her feet. I wanted to lock the door but something was telling me not to as she would find out anyway. She stormed into the room; she was not carrying anything in her hands which was a relief as the only thing that she could have used to hit us was her shoes that she wore on her feet. Yasmin wanted to see the clothes and know where we had got the money from to buy them. I showed her the clothes but without the price tags. Before we had entered the house Aisha and I made sure we took the price tags off and discarded them in a bin never to be seen again. We did this because we knew there was no way we could have returned the clothes without the tags or a receipt.

Yasmin grabbed the bags from our hands and pulled out the clothes. She was shouting and swearing. She called us slags and all of the names under the sun. Abdul was shouting too, he wanted Yasmin to hit us. I shouted back at him and told him to keep quiet. I wanted to get my own way as I knew there was a chance that Yasmin could take the clothing and throw them away without us knowing. So I stood up to her and grabbed mine and Aisha's clothes off of her. I reminded her of the fact that we were both engaged and that we were grown women now and not children. I said this because I knew this would work. She could not do anything in return because it was her and Fatima who told us that if we did get engaged we could dress and do whatever we wanted. I did not like the fact that I was using this as ammunition but it seemed to work. Yasmin gave in and said "Do not wear them all of the time, occasionally yes but Pakistani clothing is what you should wear." Aisha and I were jumping for joy; we saw Abdul's face, he looked as though he had been slapped. After Yasmin and the others had left I locked the bedroom door and Aisha and I had our very own fashion show. I felt like a million dollars in my new clothes.

29 My new look

THE FOLLOWING MORNING I woke up for college earlier than I normally would have done. I could not sleep because I was very excited. I was looking forward to wearing my new clothes and looking completely different. I could not wait to show off my new look to my friends. Just by wearing the clothes I felt confident and I could not help but look at myself in the mirror.

Aisha was also excited. But my nerves were starting to set in as the time approached for us to leave for college. I could hear someone in the bathroom, I was sure it was Yasmin. I was hoping that she would not see us and that we could quickly sneak out as Yasmin would only say nasty things to us and shatter our confidence.

I opened the door and Aisha and I tip-toed down the stairs towards the front door. Luckily Yasmin had left the main batch of keys on the kitchen table where I was able to take them without going up to her room - this was where she kept the keys after she locked up at night. As I went to open the door Yasmin came down the stairs, she had seen what we were wearing and shook her head. She said we looked like a couple of slappers. We were only wearing a pair of jeans and a top. Before she could say anything else Aisha and I walked out of the front door.

We left the house with our hair tied back as Yasmin and Fatima hated us having our hair down and as we turned a corner and we were sure we were not being watched by Yasmin any more Aisha and I untied our hair.

Walking to the college was nerve racking as I did not know what people's reactions would be. As we got to the main busy road that we always crossed I heard a beep coming from a car that went past. Aisha laughed and said "This is new, was the beep for you or was it for me?" I joked and said "It was for me, or for both of us, we are twins after all." At the entrance of the college I noticed a few looks from people that never noticed us before. Some girls were whispering in one corner which made me paranoid as I thought they were talking about us. I tried my best to hold my head up high and not to look intimidated.

Aisha and I walked to our lesson; we were walking outside when I noticed Tabassum. She did not recognise us and she walked straight past us. I called to her, she smiled and said "Wow, you both look really nice, I did not recognise you then." As we waited, more and more of our class pupils turned up. Javeria, Farida and Raheela came shortly after as we entered the computer room. They could not stop talking about how nice and different we looked. They were used to seeing us in our oversized Pakistani clothes.

Hajira was late again, she called Javeria on her mobile to say she was about ten minutes away and that she was walking up to the college. Javeria and the rest of the girls all had mobile phones. Aisha and I wanted one as they were always texting each other and had funny messages that they shared - we really felt left out. Aisha and I talked about getting a mobile phone because everyone seemed to have one and it was also a good security item. Abdul had a mobile phone which Yasmin allowed him to have but she did not want us to have one because she thought if we did have one we would have boys calling us at every hour. She saw mobile phones as forbidden things that would tempt girls into having boyfriends.

Hajira eventually arrived and she said the clothes that we were wearing really suited us. During our lesson, Henry our tutor made a very nice comment, he said that Aisha and I looked very lovely and that we reminded him of a Bollywood actress. I was not sure which one he meant until Tabassum said Aishwarya Rai and she showed him a picture in one of her magazines. Aisha and I were very flattered and I asked him how he knew of her. He said he had seen her in some of the magazines that Javeria and Tabassum always looked at in class while they should be working. I said to Javeria and Tabassum "You didn't know that Henry had eyes at the back of his head did you?" and with that he laughed.

With my new look I could see I was growing in confidence. I was noticing a lot more people in my class looking at me. I was getting attention from the opposite sex which was distracting me; I found this to be very flattering.

30 My first real crush

As WEEKS WENT on I was finding staying focused and concentrating on my lessons to be a very difficult task. My attention and thoughts were transferred from learning how to design a website to one particular person in my class. His name was Justin; he would sit across the other side of the room to me with his friend Michael. Justin was English and not Pakistani, nor was he a Muslim. I found him very attractive.

I had never really liked anyone of a different ethnicity before other than Pakistani because I had never been in that environment before. I was always told by my family never to socialise with anyone from a different ethnicity and that if I ever did it was purely for work purposes. But since getting engaged and seeing for myself what I thought Pakistani men were like I was beginning to dislike them and the attraction to them was beginning to fade.

Justin was very handsome, he was a few inches taller than me and he was very well dressed. He had lovely hair that always had a shine to it. His looks were unique; he had a kind of mystery about him which was what first attracted me to him. His smile would always make me smile and I felt like I was starting to daydream. I had a major crush on him and he had no recollection of it. This crush was affecting the way I was behaving and I became very shaky and disorientated whenever I would see him.

A couple of times while I was talking to Henry and I caught a glimpse of Justin I would forget what I was saying and what I wanted to say was not coming out right; instead I sounded very confused. Nobody knew about my feelings for Justin and I knew exactly what my friends' reactions would be. They did not see non-Pakistani men as being very attractive. I thought my friends would laugh at me and judge me if I ever were to tell them because Justin was not a Muslim, he was a non-believer - a Kafir. I could just tell the way my friends spoke that English men were not seen to be attractive to them they were always attracted to Pakistani men.

Looking around the college, I noticed that this was true as all of the boys were dating Pakistani girls and the girls were dating Pakistani boys. Thoughts were going through my mind and I was asking myself questions about why I could see a growing pattern. I came to one obvious conclusion: if by any chance one of the couples were to ever get married, then providing their parents were not strict they would agree to the marriage because ultimately they were both Muslims.

My friends' opinions of relationships were very different to mine; they were very much fixed on what their parents would like their future partner to be. I felt like they had no interest in their own future. I felt my friends left their future in the hands of their parents and they thought whatever the decision of their parents was, was the correct one for them - their parents knew best.

This computer course that we were all on felt to me like it was something for them to do, as it was two years long and within these two years they were able to live a little and they could enjoy themselves before they got married and settled down. The girls never seemed to talk about what they wanted to achieve at the end of it.

Javeria and Tabassum came across to me as dreamers; they were heavily into the Bollywood scene and always seemed to talk about the fairy tale ending. Hajira always worried about the way she looked and over time she became quite bitter. She would criticise other girls for how they looked as she thought she was the best thing since sliced bread. She referred to herself as being a 'forbidden fruit'. She would say whenever someone approached her "You can look, but you can't touch." She was quite a tease with the boys. She would lead them on and drop them just the same. Hajira thought as a Muslim she was better than the western girls, she was pure which meant she was a virgin. She had a very bitchy streak about her and if there was a girl that she did not like or she felt was a threat to her then she would call her a slag.

I was different and I was not bothered about the way I looked as I had no confidence in my appearance or myself. I only thought of myself as one of the girls in a group. Hajira was the one that seemed to stand out from our group and I just faded into the background, she was the one that attracted the men and as a result she simply could not contain her excitement. I would not get excited when a Pakistani man walked past me, instead I would just sit back and watch as my friends drooled. They were just like the men I saw in Pakistan who got excited seeing a woman; my friends were experiencing the same excitement but with these men at college.

I had experienced first-hand while I was in Pakistan what it was like being drooled over and from watching my brothers-in-law I had no desire to ever have a relationship with a Pakistani man. To me I saw them all as a bunch of vultures preying on girls. I could see from watching the boys at college that they were no different. I had a very strong opinion and perspective of them all being the same and I could not think any differently. The thought of ever going out with a Pakistani man would repulse me as I felt I was a prize and they had just won me.

I was very much attracted to Justin. I had never spoken to him but I wanted him to like me. I wanted to build up the courage to say something but the thought of rejection was too overpowering and it was pulling me back. I felt I was not very attractive and that was why he had never spoken to me. I was not sure if he liked Pakistani girls or if he was single. I was afraid he had a girlfriend as he would always disappear at lunch times and if he did like me I would turn him down because I was too afraid of my family and the Pakistani community but I could not help but liking him all the same.

I told Aisha how I felt about Justin one evening while we sat in our bedroom with the door locked, she laughed and said "I knew it". You were always so very quiet in class. She asked me why I was behaving the way I was in class and I said it was because I did not want to draw any attention to the fact that I had a crush on him. Aisha suggested that I spoke to him and we even did a role play, she pretended to be Justin but in the end it was hopeless because she was making me laugh and I knew there was no point in rehearsing because when it came down to it, I would mess it up and make a complete fool of myself. I also felt it was too late for me to approach him because it was now nearly five months since we started college and we had not even said hello to one another.

31 Dating the internet way

ONE LUNCHTIME WHILE my friends and I sat in the college canteen eating our lunch of chips, cheese and beans together, Hajira out of the blue asked us all if we fancied anyone in the college. Everyone became very shy apart from Tabassum; she was straight to the point and she did not mince her words. She said she liked a few but she was not willing to name anyone, we all laughed as she became a lovely shade of red. Farida and Raheela became very touchy and were not willing to spill the beans so they pretended to talk about something else. Hajira went on to say she liked someone. At once we all dropped our forks and stopped eating in curiosity because we were all very keen to find out who this person was. We had all noticed Hajira becoming very friendly with a Pakistani boy who was studying in the course below us. Hajira went on to say she had met this person through the internet and that he lived in a different city, we were all shocked and stunned at the same time.

I had never heard about internet dating before but the other girls had. Hajira was chatting to someone called Jamal, he was the same age her, also a Muslim but of a mixed ethnicity. Hajira said that he was half Italian and his mother had converted to Islam when she married his father. Hajira went on to tell us that he was a twin and his father was a strict Muslim. She said his twin brother was dating an Indian girl in secret. Hajira described Jamal as amazing but she did not mention what he looked like.

She said the web site was especially designed for Asian people. She said it was very good and very addictive. The site was called 'Smash Chat'. Hajira went on to say she stumbled across the site one evening when she was surfing the web. We were all very eager to find out more about this mystery man of hers. She said this was her first proper relationship and that she had never met him but she grew very fond of him as she began an online relationship with him. I asked her how long she had been chatting to Jamal and she said a couple of weeks. I then asked Hajira if she had a photograph of him as she did not mention his looks; I wanted to build a mental image of him. Her reply to me was a bit vague as I could tell she was trying to think of something to say to me. She said she did but she had lost it. I felt she had taken time to think up this reply because what she said did not come across to be very clear and she was quick in changing the subject. I got the impression she seemed a little ashamed of him.

Javeria then asked Hajira if she had spoken to him on the phone, she said yes and that he would always call her on her mobile phone at night when her family were sleeping. Hajira said she had a bedroom to herself which meant she had some privacy. She then went on to say he had brought her a mobile phone. I had noticed Hajira's new mobile phone but I just assumed it was a contract phone. Again we were all shocked to hear that Hajira had taken a gift from him and she had never seen him before. She had only been talking to him for a couple of weeks. The mobile phone was on pay-as-you-go and she said he was topping up the mobile phone for her and that it was not costing her anything. I asked her how she had received the mobile phone. She stuttered and said "He sent it to me in the post." My initial thought was she needs her head examining if she gave him her address.

This was beginning to sound worse by the minute. I was

dreading what she was going to say next. Farida tried to explain to Hajira without sounding like she was interfering that it was very dangerous giving out her address to someone who she had not known for a while. I could see Hajira beginning to feel very agitated. She was taking confrontation very badly; she became very defensive and thought we were telling her what to do and that we were judging her. I explained that this was not our intention and that we only had her safety in mind. She then lowered her guard and said "Why don't you girls give it a go? No one ever needs to find out; this is a very discrete way of meeting people of the opposite sex. You have a laugh on there and it beats chatting to people from this college."

I wanted to try the site for myself as I was lacking confidence and I wanted something interesting to do in my life. Something to take my mind off things and seeing an improvement in Hajira's confidence made me decide to give it ago. So after our lesson we all went to use the main college computer room where we saw first-hand how the site worked. Hajira logged onto 'Smash Chat' with a fake user ID. She said "You have to choose an eye-catching name that you know people would like or a name that you always wanted to be called." So she called herself 'Hot Gal' we all laughed as this was just exactly the sort of name Hajira would choose.

Once she entered the site, she sent a message on the main screen saying hello to everyone and this was also her chance to entice people to chat. Immediately, she was inundated with messages from men who wanted to chat with her. Some of the user IDs that the men were using were very rude and inappropriate. Hajira seemed to know which ones to stay away from. There were a few on there that seemed genuine so she started to type. At this point we were all huddled together by Hajira and we were drawing attention to ourselves. I could see people looking and they were curious to see what we were all looking at on the computer screen. So we all pulled up a chair and sat with some folders and note pads pretending to make notes about an assignment that we were working on. I found the internet chatting fun; an hour of chatting soon became two hours and two hours became three.

Using the internet became a regular occurrence and I found it to be rather addictive like an illegal drug. I just could not stay away from it, I found myself wanting to log onto the dating site more than I thought I would. I was on the dating site almost every day or twice a day at college on my lunch break or if I had a free period and also at home. At home I did not have a computer to call my own, instead I had to plead with Yasmin to use hers but I did not tell her the real reason why I wanted to use it instead I would say that it was for my college work.

The dating site was ninety percent targeted at the Asian community which meant there were males and females from Pakistani, Indian and Bangladeshi backgrounds logged on. I started using Kiran as my user name as I had always liked the name. By using this name I had a lot of people contacting me who wanted to chat to me. I was able to become the person I had always wanted to be. Kiran was confident, she was outgoing and she was a laugh and I felt through Kiran I was able to portray the personality which I felt I could not do as Samina.

32 Getting to know Tariq secretly

YASMIN HAD MOVED her computer from her bedroom into the front room. The reason for this was that she claimed she did not have enough room in her bedroom for the computer desk and since she left University she felt she did not need to use the computer as much as she thought she would have. Since the computer had been moved, the front room was always in use and mainly by Abdul. Abdul felt he was in charge of the computer now that Yasim did not use it and if anyone else wanted to use this computer they had to plead with him. He loved the attention he was getting and I could see he was getting a sense of power from it. Abdul would play upon this mainly when it came to Aisha and I and we knew if Abdul ever found out the real reason why we wanted to use the computer then he would have blackmailed us and made sure he made our lives a living hell.

Another college day was over and it was now the evening. Yasmin and the rest of the family were in the living room watching television, Aisha and I were in the front room. It was my turn to use the computer this evening as Aisha had used it the night before. I had been on the dating site for almost an hour when someone called Tariq contacted me.

Tariq was very polite; he said he loved my name and wanted to chat to me. I knew I did not have long on the internet this evening because I was late in logging on to the site. Yasmin was refusing to clean the kitchen and I could not bear the uncleanliness so I cleaned it for her. But this meant I only had half an hour to use the computer so I decided to make the most of my time trying to get to know Tariq.

I learned Tariq was two years older than me, he was 5ft 9 with a medium brown complexion, hazel eyes and black hair. He was attending University in Manchester, he was one of five in his family and he was a British Pakistani. Through only a few messages I felt I was getting to know Tariq very well and he did not come across to me like my brother or brothers in law - he was different, he was a gentleman he felt women were equal to men. I was asked a few questions by Tariq which I was happy to answer. He asked me my age, what I looked like, how many brothers and sisters I had and what I was studying at college. Soon it was time for me to say goodbye but before I logged off, Tariq asked me when I was going to be on-line next; I said tomorrow evening at 8pm. Tariq seemed pleased and said he would be online without fail and with that we said goodnight.

The following evening it was Aisha's turn to use the computer but she agreed to let me use it instead and true to his word Tariq was online again and I grew to like his personality very much. He started the conversation by saying "Hello beautiful" I asked Tariq why he was calling me beautiful and his reply was that he thought I had a beautiful personally and in his heart he knew my looks would match my personality. I never told Tariq about my engagement to Rizwan in Pakistan as I was very ashamed; I thought this would scare him away. Tariq never asked me if Kiran was my real name and I never asked him if Tariq was his real name. I never felt the need to as Tariq was someone I felt I could talk to and Hajira always said she never gave her real name out just in case the person she was chatting to on the other side knew her or her family.

I kept in contact with Tariq every day. Almost three months since he first contacted me, Tariq asked me for my mobile number. I knew this was coming as Hajira had been talking to three or four different people from the internet using her mobile phone. When Tariq sent me this message I was a little hesitant in replying; instead I waited and asked Aisha what her thoughts were. Aisha suggested I purchase a mobile phone but I was not sure about it because I knew Yasmin would not be happy about this; she would take the mobile phone off me and keep it for herself or she would have broken it. I felt it was very unfair because Abdul and Hamid were both younger than me and they had mobile phones. Yasmin was allowing them to use theirs.

I then had an idea, I had seen a mobile in our local mobile phone store which was £40 - it was basic and perfect. £40 was a lot of money to me and it was going to take me a few weeks to save up through my government college allowance so I decided to send a message back to Tariq to say I would like to speak to him on the internet for a couple more weeks as I felt it was too soon. Tariq was very understanding, he sent a reply back to me which gave me the impression he would wait, and as long as it made me feel at ease he was happy to chat to me via the internet. At the end of his message he added a smiley face and asked if he could have my email address. I then quickly opened another internet page and created myself an email address under the name Kiran. Once my email address was created I sent a reply back to Tariq. He seemed pleased and he said he would write me a lengthy email so I could reply back to him when I could. I had told him about my family and how strict they were and it was not always possible for me to go on the internet secretly.

It was getting late and I had been chatting to Tariq for three hours when suddenly Abdul came into the room. He swung the door open and threw himself into the room as though he had been pushed or had been listening behind the door and he thought it was a good time to surprise us. At the top of his voice he shouted "I am telling Yasim, tell me what you are doing on the computer, what are you hiding?" Abdul did this quite often, he knew by shouting and making a scene it would scare Aisha and I and Yasmin would come marching into the room demanding to know what was going on. Abdul then stamped his feet towards me and pushed me to one side to take a look at the computer screen. But I was one step ahead of him because as soon as I heard the door swing open I quickly took the dating site off but I had forgotten to take off my conversation with Tariq.

Abdul had now seen this and he was grinning from ear to ear, he became vindictive and he wanted to know who Tariq was and why I was talking to this person. He started to shout and said "Tell me or I am going to tell Yasmin." so I reluctantly told him about Tariq. Abdul automatically assumed Tariq was my boyfriend and I had been dating him secretly. It took me a while to persuade him that Tariq was just a friend but like my parents and the rest of my family it was seen to be very wrong and I should not have been chatting to anyone of the opposite sex. I pleaded with Abdul to keep his voice down because I knew Yasmin would think the same as him.

With the help of Aisha, I managed to calm him down and I begged him not to mention a word to Yasmin or anyone else in the family. Finally, Abdul agreed but asked me to tell him what Tariq and I were talking about and to keep him informed with regular updates. I knew Abdul was a gossip and could not be trusted so I decided not to tell him the truth as he would only use that against me in arguments.

Moments later Yasmin came into the room, she asked what was happening because she had heard the shouting and it was getting very late. Abdul who was now satisfied with what I had told him said to Yasmin that he wanted to use the computer now but I would not let him. I went along with his story and said "I am finished now so you can use it." and with that, I left the room making my way up to my bedroom.

33 Secretly messaging Tariq

DURING THE NEXT few weeks Tariq sent me emails on a regular basis - one or two emails every day. I would reply to him at college during my breaks. His emails were very enjoyable to read. He would tell me about his friends at university and especially his housemate Amit. Tariq had said Amit was a Hindu and was very spiritual, he liked sharing a house with him as he got a chance to learn about a different culture and religion.

I had not mentioned to any of my friends that I was chatting with Tariq via email because I felt they would judge me and maybe compare me to Hajira as they did not seem to like her very much.

In one of Tariq's emails he sent his mobile number to me and asked me if I could text him because he felt it was time for us to meet each other. So that very day while Yasmin was out visiting Fatima at her home and Abdul was out with his school friend I took my chance and sneaked out of my bedroom, downstairs and out of the back door which was unlocked to purchase myself a mobile phone.

As I was getting on the bus I was followed by Hamid, my younger brother who asked me where I was going. I lied to him and said I was meeting Javeria so we could do our coursework together. Hamid then asked what time I was coming home, I replied "I will not be long, about one hour" and with that he left. Hamid would not ask too many questions or interfere and unlike Abdul he was very understanding. He would always stick up for Aisha and I when we were targeted by Yasmin or Fatima, he also stood up to Abdul even though he was a lot younger than him. Deep down I knew I could trust Hamid and if he ever found out about my contact with Tariq he would not say a word.

Fifteen minutes had passed and I had now arrived at the mobile phone shop. I purchased the phone which I had seen a few weeks before and quickly headed back home. I hid the mobile phone in my handbag and threw the carrier bag into a nearby bin because if Yasmin was home and she saw the carrier bag in my hand she would have taken it off me to have a look to see what was inside it.

I quietly made my way up the back garden and through the back door. The back door lead straight into the kitchen and there was no sign of anyone there so I tip-toed upstairs and into my bedroom. I was greeted by Aisha, she was already in the room along with Laila and Nadia; they were cleaning the room. Aisha asked me if I was okay and I nodded. I could see from the corner of my eye that Laila had stopped what she was doing and she tried her very best to listen so she could report back to Yasim and Abdul.

I then got myself changed into a pair of red salwar kameez and I left the bedroom clutching my handbag heading for the bathroom. As I passed Yasmin's bedroom I stood at the door for a moment to try and find out if she was home but she was not, it was completely silent. I was relieved and entered the bathroom, locked the door and opened the box of my new phone in excitement. I was so happy with my new purchase and I could not wait to text Tariq. I sent a text message to Tariq and within a minute I received a reply back from him which read "I have missed you today." followed by a couple of kisses at the end of his message. I was a little taken back by this because

Tariq had never sent kisses to me before on any of his messages to me.

Thoughts started to flood my mind and I was starting to feel Tariq was falling for me. I was not sure if I was taking his text message out of context but the kisses simply reminded me of the love letters my brother-in-laws would send to my sisters or the one that Rizwan gave to me when I was in Pakistan.

I chose to ignore the kisses and replied "How are you Tariq? Have you been up to much today?" His reply to me was "I'm well sweet Kiran and I am pleased you have texted me." In the next fifteen minutes we had exchanged many messages and I was now a whiz at using my new mobile phone and writing messages. I was starting to prefer using my mobile phone over the chat site or emails. The messaging was quick and easy and I did not need to rely on the computer or risk being blackmailed by Abdul. I was starting to realise that I had gained some power from having my own mobile phone.

While I was chatting to Tariq I heard a bang on the bathroom door which was followed by shouting and cursing, it was Yasmin - she had come home. I had been so engrossed with chatting to Tariq that I had forgotten the time and I did not hear her come home. She wanted me to open the door and demanded to know what I was doing in the bathroom. I was terrified of her finding my mobile phone and I did not know what to do so I pretended to have finished using the toilet, I flushed the chain and said "I will be finished soon, just give me a minute." My mobile phone was still in my hand and I had just received another message from Tariq who asked if I would meet him on Friday. I had forgotten what day it was and Friday seemed a long way away - my mind was everywhere and all I could think about was Yasmin catching me with a mobile phone! Luckily I had turned my mobile on silent and all I needed to do now was to hide it along with my handbag.

I noticed the laundry basket; it was full to the brim so I

quickly tipped some washing out and buried my handbag and mobile phone deep inside the washing and as I did I turned the taps of the sink on full to hide any noise I was making. I then piled the remaining washing over, turned the taps off and casually opened the door. Yasmin pushed me to one side and stormed her way into the bathroom. She looked around the bathroom and at me to see if I had anything with me that I should not have had. Her fists were clenched and I could tell she wanted to hit me so I quickly left the bathroom as she turned to face me.

As I walked along the corridor I heard the floorboards creek from the opposite side so I stopped, turned and saw it was Abdul - he had been listening the entire time. He was sniggering and just like Yasmin he started to question why I was in the bathroom. I was fed up so I told Abdul to shut up and to stop stirring trouble. He followed me to my bedroom. I wanted to get in before he did so I ran the remaining steps and shut the door behind me. I had shut the door in his face and he was furious. He swung the door open, pushed me and made me fall to the floor. Aisha quickly came to my rescue and asked Abdul to leave; he was laughing and said he would make sure we never had any privacy or time to ourselves. I became very angry and emotional and shouted "I wish you were dead, I hate you!" he laughed even louder and walked out of the room slamming the door behind himself.

Abdul had scared Nadia and she was now in tears, I went to her side and told her not to worry. As she sobbed she asked me why Abdul was so awful, I was still angry and my anger turned to tears as I said "He is just like father, he was cruel and always controlling." Aisha agreed and said "He will never change."

Aisha took Nadia downstairs, she asked me if I was coming. I was still very upset so I decided to stay a while longer. My tears eventually dried up and I was feeling a little better and then I remembered my mobile phone. I waited for a few more minutes until I felt the coast was clear and Yasmin and everybody else were downstairs. I slowly and quietly opened the bedroom door and tip-toed along the corridor, carefully clutched the bathroom door handle making sure I did not make a sound. The door opened and quickly before I was seen by anyone I grabbed my mobile phone and handbag and tip-toed back to my bedroom.

Once I was inside my bedroom I viewed my mobile, I had four messages from Tariq. The first one read "Kiran I cannot wait to meet you" The second one read "I want to get to know you more Kiran, I will make sure it is a day to remember" The third one read "Kiran are you there?" and the fourth one read "Have I done something to upset you Kiran? If I have I am very sorry as it is the last thing that I would do."

I was very touched by Tariq's messages so I sent a reply back to him which read "Friday would be great Tariq, I cannot wait I must go now. I will text you later." As soon as I had sent the message I hid my mobile phone under my bed and headed downstairs to eat my dinner.

All of the family were seated in the living room with their meals in front of them in their laps watching the television. Aisha was in the kitchen plating up her food, she asked me if I had been messaging Tariq; I said yes and we are to meet up on Friday. Aisha stopped what she was doing and whispered "Friday?" I said Yes, she laughed and said "Friday is a day away."

"Oh my god!" I gasped.

34 Excited to meet Tariq

IT WAS THURSDAY evening and the eve of my meeting with Tariq. I had decided not to tell any of my friends at college about my meeting with him because deep down I knew it may compromise our friendships as meeting someone from the internet was going to the next level and most of the girls still had their traditional strict Muslim views on this. I chose to only disclose my meeting with Tariq with Aisha and she promised she would not say a word to anyone. I knew I could trust her.

I was in my bedroom looking through my wardrobe trying to pick something beautiful to wear for my meeting tomorrow when Aisha came over to me; she had been sitting on her bed working through her college assignment. She whispered to me and said "Have you found anything to wear yet for your date?", "It is not a date" I said it's a meeting between two friends, and she then said "Oh is that what you call it?" I then started to question myself and the word 'date' was playing on my mind. I realised it was a date in a way; I had met Tariq on a so-called chat site but really it was a dating site. We had exchanged mobile numbers, we were regularly messaging each other and even flirting at times. I was very excited about meeting him.

I had been searching for something to wear for half an hour and I still could not find anything suitable so I asked Aisha if I could borrow something of hers. She agreed and suggested a pair of sky-blue jeans which she had and so I tried the jeans on along with a simple white top. It was perfect as the weather was warm so I did not need to wrap myself up too much.

I wanted to wear something casual but not suspicious to Yasmin. She always questioned me whenever I wore something that she found revealing or tight fitting and she would automatically assume I was meeting someone of the opposite sex and not attending college. I did not want to arouse her suspicions on this occasion even though I knew meeting Tariq was wrong in my family's eyes. If I were to get caught I would have been sent to Pakistan immediately and married.

I could hear footsteps outside the bedroom door so I quickly gathered my clothing and threw them into my wardrobe and began to read through my college file. The bedroom door suddenly swung open - it was Yasmin. She never knocked on the door instead she would force her way in with no respect for our privacy. She shouted at the top of her voice and said "Who's turn is it to make chapatis tonight?" Aisha looked at me quickly and then at Yasmin without saying a word because she knew it was my turn.

I looked at Yasmin and said "Is the curry ready?" She looked at me like I was something stuck under her shoe and said "Yes it's ready, get yourself downstairs now!" So I quickly closed my file and asked her how many chapatis she and Aisha wanted. They both answered two so I made a mental note and headed downstairs to ask the others. Abdul decided to be awkward and said he wanted four and then he changed his mind and said three and then back to four again, he would often to this.

When the chapatis were ready, I called everyone to the kitchen to eat. Yasmin started to plate the curry while everyone helped themselves to the chapatis. I took my share of the curry and chapatis that I had made and sat down at the kitchen table. Everyone else took their meal into the living room where they sat eating it in front of the television. Laila and Nadia were never allowed to sit on the sofa; instead they were seated on the floor while Yasmin, Abdul and Hamid all sat on the sofa.

As I was eating my meal Aisha came and sat beside me and said "You need to be more careful."

"Careful?" I said, "Yes," she said "I have noticed you have not been paying attention to what is happening at home. It was your turn to make chapatis this evening but you forgot and it lead to Yasmin coming upstairs angry and having a go at us again." I stopped eating and apologised to Aisha as I knew I was in the wrong and I should have not let my excitement over chatting to Tariq cause me to forget my duties. Whenever Yasmin was angry she would always blame the both of us for something she was not happy about.

I had now finished my meal and it was nearly 9.00pm, Tariq had sent a message earlier to say he would be meeting me near college at 8.30 in the morning so I wanted to have an early night as I knew I would find it difficult to sleep. I headed upstairs to get myself ready for bed. Aisha stayed behind because it was her turn to wash the dishes and clean the kitchen. Laila and Nadia were also going to sleep but it was far too early for Abdul or Yasmin. They would often stay awake watching Indian soaps until the early hours or they would be on the telephone talking to Fatima about the day's happenings. They would always say nasty things about Aisha and I which lead to Fatima threatening to stop our college and to take us to Pakistan to be married. Hamid was sensible, he would go to sleep at a reasonable hour; he was not really interested in watching soaps, instead he would talk to his friends on his mobile phone or he would do his homework and have an early night.

As I walked quickly up the stairs, I could hear sounds coming from the bathroom and as I got closer to the door I could hear it was Laila and Nadia; they were brushing their teeth and getting themselves ready for bed so I took this opportunity to quickly run into the bedroom while no one was there to say goodnight to Tariq. It was a little difficult to try to retrieve my mobile phone from under my bed because I had pushed it too far. I was worried about getting caught and someone finding it so I had to move my bed to one side. My bed was a small single bed and it was easy to move.

When I had my phone, there were a few messages from Tariq and my palms began to get warm and sweaty with excitement and nerves. The excitement was from receiving the messages and the nerves came from the possibility of getting caught. One by one I quickly opened each message and as I did I found myself smiling. Tariq had said he was very excited to meet me and he did not think he would sleep tonight. He asked me if I felt the same and he was pleased he had contacted me, the last message wished me sweet dreams followed by two kisses.

Without hesitation I sent a reply back to him and apologised for not replying to him sooner due to my commitments at home. I said I could not wait to meet him too and ended my message with "See you at 8.30 in the morning around the corner from the petrol station on Broom street. I will be wearing sky blue jeans with a white top, you will not be able to miss me! I will text you when I leave in the morning goodnight x x" As soon as the message was sent I moved my bed back to where it originally was and buried my mobile phone under some clothes in my wardrobe. I moved a handful of my college books and files in front of the door in the hope that nobody would discover my secret. I then peacefully changed into a pair of loose fitted salwar kameez and lay in my bed hoping to fall asleep.

35 Finally meeting Tariq

THE DAY HAD arrived for my meeting with Tariq and I was feeling very tired. I was the first one up this morning and I had woken up before my alarm sounded. I felt happy because I could not wait to leave the house and finally meet Tariq face to face instead of communicating by phone. Laila and Nadia were both starting to stir; the morning light was bright and it was shining on them. I quietly picked up my towel and headed for the bathroom to freshen up.

When I got back, Aisha was awake and she was sitting on her bed waiting for me to return so she could use the bathroom. Laila and Nadia were both now awake and talking amongst themselves. I then started to iron my clothes and as I did Laila asked me what I was going to do at college today. I said I was designing a web page for my coursework and it was going to take up most of my day. She seemed very interested and asked if she could see it when I had completed it so I agreed. I then changed into the outfit that I had decided to wear and I began to dry my hair.

Twenty minutes later Aisha came back into the room and Laila and Nadia both ran to get into the bathroom before Abdul got there because they knew he would take his time and they would be late for school.

As Aisha made her bed she commented on the way I looked, she said she thought I looked wonderful. She wanted to know if she could meet Tariq too. I said yes because Aisha was going to walk to college with me and I did not want to leave her while I met Tariq. My excitement was starting to turn into nervousness and I had butterflies in my stomach; having Aisha by my side would make me feel at ease.

It was soon time for us to leave; we chose not to have any breakfast before we left because we knew Abdul would cause trouble for us by being verbally abusive and commenting on the way we were dressed. He hated us wearing western clothing and he would make sure Yasmin had something to say about it. Instead, we sneaked out of the house without saying goodbye to anyone. As we walked further from the house we untied our hair because that was the style we preferred.

I then took my mobile phone out which I had hid in my jeans pocket. I wanted to text Tariq to say we were on our way but I had already received a message from him to say he had arrived and he was waiting for me.

Aisha said she was feeling nervous too and hoped we would not be seen by any of our family members or people who knew us. My heart began to sink and I felt sick to my stomach of the thought of Kabir seeing us or one of his friends. Kabir would take Wasim and Ali to a local school near to the college. This was a special school for children with learning difficulties. Shazia was staying at home looking after her third child, Sadia - she was one year old. Over the years Shazia became very tired and her health was suffering; she would say she could not take care of the children by herself because they were a handful and Kabir was eventually forced into taking some responsibility.

All three of her children had autism, Wasim had Mild Autism but Ali and Sadia both suffered from a more severe form.

We were nearly there when my mobile phone began to vibrate. I was nervous and it was slipping out of my sweating hand. Tariq had sent a message to say he could see me and he liked what he was seeing. He said I was walking very elegantly and he hoped I liked him too. I could not see Tariq so I asked him what car he was driving. He said he was driving a white Nissan Micra. I saw his car, it was a couple of meters away from me. Aisha started to giggle and asked me if I was okay. She said she thought she was walking with a tomato. I was not feeling okay, my cheeks were burning up and my hands were sweating. I took a deep breath and slowly walked the remaining steps towards the car and hoped I would not lose my balance and fall.

Tariq lowered the passenger side window and said hello. I lowered my head to look at him and I was pleasantly surprised, he was better looking than I had imagined. His complexion was golden, his eyes were a bright hazel and his physique was to die for. He looked like a model from a magazine and as he spoke I was taken aback by his voice - it was deep but gentle. He said he was pleased to have finally have met me and he was amazed on how alike Aisha and I were. Tariq stepped out of his car and introduced himself to Aisha. The smile on my face became even bigger when I saw him standing in front of me. He was a few inches taller than me, his body was very muscular, the white T-shirt he was wearing really suited him, it was tight fitted which was a bonus for me because I could see his abs and they really looked great. He had paired his T-Shirt with Navy blue jeans and I felt he had matched his outfit to mine which I found very touching because it showed he had put thought into what he was wearing.

I told Tariq that Aisha and I would be going to our lesson soon and it would be over in a couple of hours. I did not want Tariq to feel like I was neglecting him so I asked him if he wanted to come along with us to the college and wait in the college canteen or if he wanted to have a look around the area. Tariq said he was feeling a little hungry and he wanted to freshen up after the long drive so he asked if he could go into the college. Aisha nudged me with her elbow and whispered "Are you sure?

He may attract unwanted attention?" It was nearly the end of term and the college was always very quiet at this time of year so I said "Sure, it will be fine."

As we walked to the entrance, Aisha walked slightly ahead of Tariq and I as I could sense she was worried about someone seeing us. We were early and I knew our friends would not have arrived yet. I thought Tariq was everything that I had imagined him to be. I hoped our friends did not see him because I thought they would be jealous and judge me.

As we all walked into the college, I showed Tariq where the toilets were and then I walked him down to the canteen. He laughed as we walked down the stairs, and said "So, is this the famous canteen that you always talk about?" I became a little shy and said "Yes, a lot happens here when it is busy." He looked at me and shook his head a little as if to say he thought I was pulling his leg. Aisha went on to say "Just wait and see, it is like a soap opera at times." Tariq just smiled.

There were only a handful of people in the canteen and the café was open for breakfast orders so Tariq asked if we wanted anything to eat or drink. Aisha and I both shook our heads, "We must go now, our lesson will be starting soon and we cannot be late." Tariq understood and we said goodbye.

On the way to our lesson I asked Aisha what she thought about Tariq. She said she really liked him and she thought he was kind-hearted - and he looked good too. I smiled at her and said "He is isn't he..."

As we approached the computer room there was a queue outside the door; everyone was waiting to go in as our teacher Henry had not arrived yet. As Aisha and I walked to the back of the queue I heard someone call my name. It was Tabassum; she was seated on the floor with Farida, Javeria and Raheela. We walked towards them and asked if they knew where Henry was. Javeria said he was on his way. The girls were in conversation about what they had watched on television last night when Tabassum said she thought Aisha and I looked very beautiful today; they asked if our clothes were new. I went on to say I was wearing Aisha's jeans but my top was new. Tabassum always commented on what we were wearing, she often said she liked our dress sense. Moments later, Henry arrived and we all entered the computer room to begin our lesson.

Half an hour into our lesson Hajira arrived, she was late as usual so she tried her very best to sneak into the lesson without Henry seeing her but it did not work. She had been caught out the moment she pulled up a chair to sit beside me. Henry was standing behind her and said "Glad you could make it this morning." Hajira just laughed and said "I am sorry, my bus was late again." I could see the expression on Henry's face that he did not believe her, he said "You may need to think about catching a different bus next time." Hajira's laugh turned into a frown which I found very amusing to watch.

Our lesson was nearly over and I could feel my mobile phone vibrating in my pocket. I had received a message from Tariq; he asked me how my lesson had gone. He was feeling a little out of place in the canteen because it was beginning to get busy and people were starting to stare at him. I had a feeling that this would happen because Tariq did not fit in. I sent a message back to him to say "You are a star, people are bound to stare because they have not seen anyone as good looking as you before."

Hajira asked me if everything was okay and who I was messaging. I could see from the corner of my eye that Farida, Javeria, Raheela and Tabassum had all now stopped what they were doing and looking in my direction waiting to hear what I would say. I hesitated while I thought about what to say, it was nearly lunch time and I had forgotten that all of the girls would be heading down to the canteen to have their lunch so I chose to tell them the truth.

Javeria and Tabassum became very excited and could

not wait to meet Tariq. Raheela and Farida had a sort of disappointed look on their faces which felt to me like I had done something terribly wrong and Hajira simply did not say a word. I felt Hajira may have been jealous of me because she had been chatting to Jamal for many months now and she still had not introduced him to us.

The lesson was now over and we all headed towards the canteen. Tabassum had her arm linked with mine as we walked and asked me if Tariq did not mind them meeting him. I had not asked Tariq if it was fine for me to bring my friends along to meet him but I was sure it was not going to be a problem so I said it would be fine.

I entered the canteen first followed by Tabassum, Aisha and the rest of my friends. I could see the canteen was rather busy and Tariq was seated on the far left. I walked towards him with confidence and as I stopped by Tariq I could see a gang of Pakistani boys and girls looking in my direction, they were huddled up together and were talking. Tariq smiled and stood up to greet me, he touched one of my hands and said "How are you?" I said I was fine and I had brought my friends along to meet him, he was happy and I began to introduce my friends to him.

Tabassum and Javeria really warmed to Tariq and so did Hajira but Raheela and Farida seemed to hesitate and only spoke when Tariq spoke to them. I could see from Raheela's face and body language that she felt awkward and she did not want to be seen speaking to someone of the opposite sex.

We had been talking for almost two hours and the canteen was now virtually empty. Raheela and Farida decided to leave first followed by Tabassum and Javeria, they had planned to go shopping in town. Hajira was also getting ready to leave; she was meeting Jamal so they all said their goodbyes and left together. I could not help but feel they were leaving together for a reason - they wanted to talk about Tariq and I. Tariq asked

Aisha and I if we fancied showing him the local area as he had never been to our city before, we had the afternoon to ourselves so we agreed.

Aisha and I were extremely nervous about getting into Tariq's car just in case someone were to see us so I told Tariq how I felt. He understood and asked me where the local car accessory shop was. I asked him why but he chose not to tell me. Instead he said he would tell me when he returned. Tariq was soon back and returned with some black sunshades. He explained that he was going to put a sunshade on the passenger side and back two windows. The sunshades were dark enough to hide a person so we would not be seen by anyone looking into the car. This was a huge relief and Aisha and I both decided to sit in the back of the car because the windows were a lot smaller and the sunshades covered most of the window. Tariq did not seem to mind, which made me like him even more.

During the drive we passed many shops. I found myself sounding like a terrible tour guide. Tariq and Aisha teased me about this and said I would be useless if it was my profession. I laughed, but I knew I really did not have a clue about street names or where we were because I had seen so little of my own town myself. Aisha chose to stay quiet because I knew she was in the same boat as me.

I glanced forward from time to time and I could see Tariq looking at me through the rear view mirror of the car. He would give me a cheeky smile which sent my heart racing.

After some thought I decided to tell Tariq my real name because I wanted to be honest with him and I was beginning to like him more than a friend. When I told Tariq, I thought he would have been hurt by this or he may have been angry but he was not. I was extremely surprised at his reaction as he said he knew all along that Kiran was not my real name. I asked him how did he know and he said he just had a feeling but he was waiting for me to tell him.

It was nearly 4pm and time for us to go home. On the way back to the college Tariq asked if we wanted a lift home instead. I discussed this briefly with Aisha and asked Tariq if it was okay for him to drop us off a few streets away because we did not want be seen by family or neighbours. Tariq agreed and said that would be the safest way. Soon we had arrived and it was time for me to say goodbye, Aisha stepped out of the car first leaving me alone with Tariq for the very first time. He turned to face me, gave me a warm hug and said he had a wonderful day. He asked me if I wanted to meet up with him again and this time he would take me to the cinema. I said yes without hesitation because I had become very fond of him and I knew he felt the same way about me.

Aisha and I were ready to leave and before we did, we tied our hair back up. I turned my mobile phone on to silent and hid it in the left side of my jeans pocket. Tariq commented on this and asked if this is what we did on a daily basis. I said yes, it was like we were living two different lives. Tariq had a sad expression on his face and asked me to message him when I was safely home. I found that very heart warming and so I agreed.

36 Falling in love with Tariq

WHEN AISHA AND I arrived home, Yasmin was in the hallway talking on the telephone to Imran in Pakistan, she seemed to be laughing and joking with him which on this occasion stopped her from making a remark as we walked past her. We were then closely followed by Laila who asked us where we had been. I had told Laila that morning that we were going to college but she always seemed to try her best to catch us out if she could. It felt like she was a spy hired by Yasmin and Abdul. I became rather angry and said "Laila, go away and leave us alone." but she was not listening to me, instead she ignored me and skipped in front of Aisha and I to get into the bedroom before we did.

I wanted to send a message to Tariq but it was not safe for me to do so. Laila was watching me with her beady eyes and I could hear Yasmin call my name from the bottom of the stairs. Moments later I heard loud footsteps heading towards our room, it was Yasmin. She shouted in Urdu and began to use foul language. She wanted me to speak to Rizwan. Imran had invited Rizwan to their house so he could speak to me. I was not willing to speak to him, I hated him. Yasmin lowered her voice as she tried to make me understand why it was so important for me to get to know him. It was starting to look very bad on our family whenever I would refuse to speak to him. I was not prepared to budge and Yasmin pleaded with me to change my mind. She then came to realise I was not going to speak to him so she headed back downstairs. I slowly followed behind her to hear what she would say. Yasmin apologised to Rizwan for my rude behaviour and said "She will change her mind soon so do not worry about it." I shook my head in disgust and headed back to my room.

While I was getting changed into a pair of unflattering salwar kameez, Laila and Aisha were leaving the bedroom. The coast was now clear for me to message Tariq. I was alone so I quickly sent a message to him to say I was fine and I told him what had just happened.

Tariq replied back to me soon after with "Tell Rizwan to hop it! And I miss you." I giggled to myself and sent a message back to him saying "I miss you too, take me away from all of this." Tariq sent a lengthy message back to me and said "You are a wonderful, kind-hearted person and I wish you did not have to put up with your family treating you the way they do, try to be brave and God willing it may work out for the better soon." I wanted to believe him but I could not see my life changing, instead I could see it heading the same way as my sisters. Tears started to roll down my face as I sent a message back to him saying "I love you, thank you for being there for me. x" and then within a minute or two I received a message back from Tariq to say he loved me too and he would try his very best to make me happy starting with showing me a little of the outside world that I had been missing such as the cinema, shopping and eating out. My tears soon dried up as we exchanged a couple more messages.

It was time for me to go downstairs and I could hear my family all heading for the kitchen because the evening meal was now ready.

After I had eaten, I did the washing up and the cleaning of the kitchen and headed back upstairs to my room. Laila and Nadia were in bed trying to complete their homework and Aisha was putting her belongings away. I was eager to hear Tariq's voice again so I took my mobile phone into the bathroom. I called Tariq who was surprised that I had called and asked me if everything was okay. I whispered and said it was the usual and I missed hearing his voice. I asked him when he wanted to meet up with me as I had a plan. Tariq asked me what my plan was. I explained that I had an idea.

It was now the summer break and college was over but I wanted Yasmin and the rest of my family to think Aisha and I still had college for a few weeks so we can go out and enjoy ourselves. Tariq said that he had finished University now and he was free do as he pleased. I was very excited to hear this and asked Tariq if he could pick Aisha and I up at 8.30am Monday morning.

Tariq agreed and laughed, he said I was very wicked but could see where I was coming from. If he was in the same position as me he would have done the exact same thing. I ended my conversation by telling Tariq I loved him and he said he felt the same about me. I quickly went back into the bedroom to tell Aisha about what I had planned but I was unable to do so as Laila and Nadia were in the room so I took out my note pad and wrote it down. Aisha pretended to ask questions about our college work to disguise the fact that we were secretly communicating about something else and she wrote back "Yes, I cannot wait!"

I felt like I had finally gained some freedom that I had never experienced before. Through the years I had seen people at school discussing their holidays and the plans they had over the summer break and now I had something to look forward to. This was my turn to have a holiday and a chance to enjoy myself, I could not wait for the next few weeks of freedom and fun.

Over the weekend I messaged and spoke with Tariq whenever it was possible for me to do so. On Saturdays Yasmin would make her weekly trip to the supermarket with Abdul, Laila and Nadia and I would make the most of my time talking to Tariq discussing many topics including music, films and food.

On Sundays Yasmin would always go to Fatima's house and she would also take Laila and Nadia along with her, they would spend the day there and Abdul would go to Shazia and Kabir's house. Abdul was interested in satellite television and he would go to a local Car boot sale with Kabir to pick up bargains. I never found Hamid to be a threat to me as he would always mind his own business.

On this particular Sunday when Hamid was home, he walked in on me talking to Tariq in the living room but he didn't seem to mind. I stopped talking expecting to get a reaction but instead he said "Sorry I did not know you were here, I will come back later." Hamid then left the room; I ran after him and asked him not to mention to anyone that he had seen me with a mobile phone and he promised not to.

The following day was Monday and everyone in the family assumed we were at college as usual. Aisha and I got dressed in our casual western clothing and headed out of the front door to meet Tariq who was parked a few streets away like before. Tariq greeted us with a warm smile and a hug. He asked us what we wanted to do that day and what time we were due back home.

I asked Tariq if we could go to the cinema as we had never visited the cinema before to watch a film. Tariq asked if there was a cinema nearby, I said there was but I did not want to go there just in case we were seen by someone who knew us so he asked if we were happy about travelling to a cinema out of our city - it would also be a road trip. Aisha and I both looked at each other and said "Yes!" in excitement, we were acting like children but it was the only way we could relax and be ourselves without the fear of someone seeing us and telling our family.

Tariq knew how afraid Aisha and I were of getting caught so he took a different route out of the city; this route was longer but he said it was for the best and we could also have something to eat on the way.

During the journey, Tariq never asked us for any money towards the petrol for his car or for the food, he was a true gentleman and offered to pay for anything we wanted. We were all getting on very well. Tariq had a collection of Bangra, Bollywood and R'n'B CDs. We took it in turns to play the music we wanted to listen to and soon we had arrived at the cinema. I remember feeling overwhelmed seeing the large film posters that were displayed everywhere we turned and the large cinema screen simply blew me away.

Once our cinema experience was over we were all feeling hungry so we decided to get something to eat. I asked Tariq what his favourite place was to eat and he mentioned a place called Chicken Hut. Tariq was health conscious and said he would eat chicken at least 5 times a week. I could see from Tariq's physique that eating a lot of chicken was not doing him any harm. The menu for Chicken Hut was large and there was a lot to choose from. Tariq recommended a chicken fillet burger, and said the chicken was very healthy and it was filling. Aisha and I had never had a chicken burger before and we were very keen to try it for ourselves. At home my family never believed in having anything other than home cooked meals so we never had the experience of a take-away meal before.

A few minutes later our chicken fillet burgers were ready and I began to eat mine. The taste was unbelievable - Tariq was right, the chicken was delicious.

After we finished our meal, Tariq offered to show us around his home town so we went on a drive for a couple of hours. I was amazed to see so many Pakistani people in one area of the town and Tariq said his family knew a lot of them. I remember thinking I had seen a similar scene before when I visited Pakistan. I was feeling a little uncomfortable and was relieved when it was time for us to head back.

37 Receiving a call that would change my life forever

AISHA AND I saw Tariq every day during the following week, apart from the weekend. He would always travel to see us and meet us at the same place. Seeing Tariq every day was like a dream come true, we could not imagine spending time during the summer break at home doing nothing but cooking, cleaning and generally being controlled by Yasmin and Abdul.

It was mid-week and we were all on another road trip. This time we were eating our lunch in a Pakistani restaurant when I received a call from Hamid who said Yasmin was furious, she was shouting and cursing me. I did not understand so I asked him why. Hamid went on to say "She has found out that you have been chatting to someone called Tariq, she thinks you have been seeing this person and he is your boyfriend." I could not speak; my throat became dry, I was speechless. Terror overtook me and all I could think about was not going home that day because I knew Yasmin would have spread what she had found out with the help of Abdul to the rest of the family. I could not understand how she had seen my emails, Hamid said "Abdul told her, he hacked into your email account and showed Yasmin the entire contents with great pleasure." I could sense from Hamid's voice he was angry too, he went on to say "She is blaming me, they all are."

"Why are they blaming you?" I said. He replied "She thinks I knew about this and kept it quiet for you, she thinks this Tariq is my friend or something." I tried my best to keep my voice down and not to draw attention to our table but I found it very difficult because Hamid was shouting, he seemed angry and afraid.

As I talked to Hamid I could see Aisha had a worried look on her face and so I walked out of the restaurant with the phone to my ear.

I was quickly followed by Aisha and Tariq. Aisha knew I was talking to someone from home and asked me if it was Hamid. I nodded and she asked to speak to him. I passed my phone over to her and told Tariq what had just happened. Tariq was just as shocked as I was and asked me if there was anything he could do. I knew there was nothing that Tariq could have done to change what had happened but all I could say was "I am not going back home."

Aisha then stopped talking to Hamid and said it was terrible. She was stuttering and shaking as she said "Kamran and Kabir are at the house and they have said they are going to kill us both when we get home. Hamid has said Kabir has a wooden stick in his hand." Then my mobile phone began to ring again and it was Hamid again, he said "Fatima and Yasim are both in your room searching your belongings."

"Searching my belongings?" I said and he went on to say "Yes, because they want to find clues to who this Tariq really is and what exactly both of you have been up to." I asked Hamid where he was speaking from and he said he was in the living room while everyone else was upstairs. I then said to Hamid that Aisha and I were not going to come home, Hamid agreed and said that was the best option because everyone was very angry and something terrible would have happened if we did go home.

I asked Hamid if he was okay and I apologised for getting him involved. He said he was not okay because he was seen as our accomplice and being accused of things he had not done, but he could take care of himself and he then said he would call again later.

Tariq walked Aisha and I to the car and then he went back into the restaurant to settle the bill. While Aisha and I sat in the car waiting for Tariq to return we discussed the options we had and what we were going to do but there were no options, we clearly had nowhere to go. We could not go back home because our family would have badly beaten us and then they would have sent us to Pakistan on the next flight to be married - they would have left us there to teach us a lesson. We could not stay with any of our friends because all of their parents had traditional views and values so they would never have approved of us staying in their home; it would have also been the first place Fatima and Yasmin would have looked to find us anyhow.

As we were talking, my mobile phone began to ring once more. I answered it thinking it was Hamid but it was Fatima, she had taken Hamid's mobile phone off him and she wanted to speak to me asking when we were coming home. I told her that we were never going back home. Fatima began to cry and pleaded with me to think about our parents and the family's reputation. I knew our parents' names would have been brought into this so I chose to ignore it. She then started to question me and wanted to know who Tariq was and what my relationship was with him. I did not reply to her questions and asked her to calm down, she then started to swear at Tariq and I could hear Kamran in the background saying he was going to kill him. Fatima was hysterical - she was cursing Tariq's family and saying his parents were bad people. I could not bear speaking to Fatima any longer and I was about to hang up on her when she asked to speak to Aisha. Aisha turned the mobile phone onto loud speaker so I could hear what she had to say. Fatima asked Aisha if Tariq was her boyfriend, she said no and then she begged Aisha to come home. Aisha also said no and Fatima started to cry once more, she sobbed and pleaded for us to return home before anyone found out that we had left; she tried to use emotional blackmail. She was saying how Aisha was more of a daughter to her than a sister and how she had raised her from the moment she was born. Aisha was getting emotional and refused to speak to Fatima any longer, she handed the mobile phone over to me and asked me to say goodbye. I was now in tears as I said goodbye to Fatima and then I ended the conversation.

Moments later, Tariq returned and asked if we were okay and if any circumstances had changed. I told him about what Fatima and Hamid had said and what the consequences were if we turned home. Tariq was saddened to hear this and he offered us support. He offered to let us stay temporarily at his university accommodation because he knew we had nowhere else to go and he feared for our safety. Aisha and I were heartbroken to have lost our family over a decision between our freedom and our family's years of tradition.

We were extremely thankful to Tariq for supporting us. I felt free at last; the shackles that Aisha and I had worn our entire lives were now finally broken. I took a couple of deep breaths and imagined running free without looking back. The heavy weight of my family's influence was no longer a burden, preventing me from moving. There was no pull at my arm or someone telling me what I was doing was wrong. I could finally breathe on my own and I knew I had made the right decision with my heart as my guide.

38 Breaking Free

THE TIME WAS approaching 4pm. It had been an hour since I ended my conversation with Fatima although it was mainly a one-way conversation - her way. During the call I had struggled to get myself heard while Fatima was shouting and crying. I was still clutching my mobile phone and with my eyes fixated on the screen, all I could do was watch as another missed call appeared and was logged onto the screen.

I had sixteen missed calls in total now, all from the same person, Hamid. But I knew it could not have been Hamid calling me but Fatima. Aisha and I were both seated in the back of Tariq's car, he was driving us to his University accommodation. Aisha was sobbing as she stared at my mobile phone, it was ringing again and she asked me if I was going to answer it. I told her no, I knew there was no point in speaking to Fatima, she would only try to persuade me to change my mind. My decision had been made and I did not want her poisoning my mind and making me feel worse than already was.

My mobile stopped ringing and another missed call was logged onto the screen. Moments later it began to ring again, it seemed as though Fatima had my number on speed dial and was not prepared to give up until I answered her call. Aisha screamed "answer it!", I looked at her and calmly said "no" she looked at me as though I was heartless. I snapped at her and said "You answer the phone then, it won't be Hamid!" She grabbed the phone out of my hand and answered the call; there was vulnerability in her voice as she said "Hello". I could hear Fatima, she was so loud and aggressive and screamed "Why were you ignoring my calls, you bitch?" Aisha was stunned and ended the call. I looked at Aisha and shook my head, "Now do you know why I chose not to answer her calls, you know it's always going to be Fatima and Yasmin in control, they are always going to use Hamid as they know we will speak to him. They use Hamid to get to us, why do you think they are blaming him for us leaving. I feel so sorry for him, it's not his fault."

Tariq intervened, saying "I think it may be best if you switched your mobile phone off for a while or just until we reach the accommodation, this may help the situation because at the moment tensions are at a high and your sister is trying her best to speak to you. She knows you may answer her and return home. There is currently a way for her to communicate with you. But if you switch your phone off she will have time to think about her actions and this will also give you and Aisha some peace." I took Tariq's advice and switched my mobile phone off. There was silence at last. I glanced in the rear view mirror at Tariq who gave me a comforting smile which assured me I had done the right thing. I moved towards Aisha and embraced her, she did not say a word but accepted my sisterly affections.

Aisha and I had fallen asleep. We were woken up by the sound of Tariq's voice, "We have arrived." he said. I rubbed the sleep out of my eyes and looked at him, bewildered. I got up to gaze out of the car window. Tariq had parked opposite a terraced house with a blue door. I was exhausted; my mobile phone was still in my hand. I turned it on and stepped out of the car. As we walked up to the front door of the house, Tariq explained his housemates had moved out and we had the entire house to ourselves for a few weeks. Walking into the house felt strange and I was feeling afraid in some way. I felt I was doing something wrong and I should have been at home this very moment and not entering a house which was alien to me.

The house was modest, with a bathroom, kitchen and three small bedrooms. Tariq escorted us to his bedroom and said he did not mind moving into one of the other rooms while Aisha and I stayed at the house. As I peered through each of the bedrooms I noticed there were no female touches to any of the rooms. Tariq's bedroom was above the kitchen, the walls and the ceiling were painted magnolia, and the carpet was grey. The room was spacious with a large window which filtered light through. From glancing around the room I could tell Tariq was a tidy person who took a keen interest in cleanliness. His double bed was neatly made and was positioned in the centre of the room, with a bookcase on the left and some barbells and fitness equipment on the right. Everything was in its rightful place.

I entered Tariq's room and flopped onto the edge of his bed with a sigh and glanced around at his room. As I did so, I felt my mind wander away from what was in front of me and turn to what I had left behind. My belongings were not of concern to me but my family were. I began to doubt myself for running away and for making Aisha feel like she had no choice but to run away with me. I felt awful as if I was a bad person and deep down I felt I had made a terrible mistake. I imagined myself in Fatima's shoes and thought about how she must be feeling. I was hurting her, she was in tears when she spoke to me but I felt she was the one in the wrong and the one who was being selfish towards me. Maybe Fatima was genuinely concerned for us but she just had a funny way of showing it. She had a lot to deal with when our parents suddenly passed away as she and Yasmin felt responsible for us and maybe Aisha and I were to blame, we may have not made things easier for them both. I felt I owed them both for taking care of us. My heart was torn to pieces. I was struggling to differentiate between my feelings which I thought were right and the family's dynamics which I have always believed to be wrong.

Suddenly my thoughts were broken by the ringing of my mobile phone, I was receiving an incoming call but it was a number I did not recognise. I hesitated briefly and then I curiously answered the call and to my surprise it was the police. I felt a little afraid at first as it was a call from our local police station which was a walking distance from our home. I was asked by the police officer on the other end of the line to confirm my name, then if I was in any danger and if Aisha was with me. I answered no to the danger part and yes to Aisha being with me. The officer then went on to explain that Yasmin and Fatima had reported us as missing people, that we had disappeared suddenly hours earlier without notifying any of our immediate family and friends. Yasmin and Fatima were adamant we had been abducted. I could not help but smirk as Yasmin and Fatima had gone to great lengths to make up a story and portray a false impression of themselves what had really happened.

The police officer asked a number of routine questions which I was happy to answer. One of which was our location, I told her where we were and that we had been forced to leave home as we were afraid of going back. I informed her that we were threatened and that there was no way Aisha and I were going to return home, we were afraid for our safety. She then went on to ask if we could make our way to the police station to formally answer a few more questions. I looked over to Tariq who nodded to say it was fine.

It was now the evening; Aisha and I had barley time to settle into our new surroundings when we were due back on the road again and returning to our hometown. It was cold and we had not eaten. Twenty minutes into the journey Tariq stopped at a service station to refuel and we all ate a quick snack at a nearby

McDonald's restaurant.

Aisha and I had never been away from home and family for this length of time before; it was dark and the "outside world" looked daunting at night. As we reached our destination I could feel my legs tremble, I was on edge and I felt a family member had seen us. The streets were well lit and takeaways which I had not noticed before during the day seemed to have appeared out of nowhere with bright flashing lights.

Tariq pulled up outside the police station. Aisha and I nervously stepped out of the car and quickly entered the station. We were greeted by the same police officer who I had spoken to. She escorted Aisha and I into an interview room. As I sat down I noticed a missing persons report relating to us and on the top of the report was an unflattering school photograph of Aisha and I. I could not contain my laughter as I took a closer look; Aisha nudged me in a gesture to make me stop. I was struggling believe, Aisha and I were actually missing people!

The police officer had a number of routine questions to ask. She then went on to say she had been given a list of contact numbers for our college friends which Yasmin had put together. She had called our friends who did not have any information of our whereabouts. I informed her that Aisha and I had never disclosed any details about our family life to any of my friends as we felt they would not understand. I explained I had no one to turn to but Aisha, we just had one another. I then went on to explain further how isolated we felt in our home, our forced engagements and how it made us feel. The police officer listened and made notes. As I explained our situation and concerns I hoped she understood as all my life I felt people would not understand. I explained how terrified we were of going back home "we have been threatened many times." I went on to say. We have experienced emotional and psychological pressure from my entire family including the extended family and on numerous occasions even physical violence from my sisters and in the past from our brothers in-law but now since they have found out about Tariq they have threatened to beat me very badly including Aisha and Tariq.

The police officer was sympathetic and reassured us that our case was not unique. She had come across a number of similar cases in her career and she assured me that steps would be taken to ensure our safety. Once the interview had concluded the police officer asked if we would consider carrying out an injunction against the family members who Aisha and I felt were a threat to us. I had never heard about an injunction before so the police officer explained it to me. Aisha and I discussed this and felt it was the right thing to do. I felt terrible for going ahead with it but I knew it was for our safety.

The police officer seemed concerned, she asked if we had enough money to live off and advised that we did not live close to the family home. Aisha and I hoped to study at the local university but it was far too close to the house. The officer advised that we moved away and studied at an alternative university. This was what Aisha and I intended to do and for money we were going to live off our student loans for a brief period and then we would find part time jobs for support. The police officer seemed satisfied with the report she had filled in and advised us that if we had any problems with our family to contact the direct number for her. Aisha and I were grateful for the help and support we gained from the police and headed out of the police station to the car. Tariq asked if the police were helpful; I explained what we had discussed and what was decided. He felt it was also the right thing to do.

39 Taking a Risk

HAMID CALLED ME secretly whenever he could during the next couple of weeks. He would ask how Aisha and I were getting on. On this particular occasion when he called, I asked him if I could arrange a day for us to make a visit to the house when no one else was at home so we could collect some important documents such as birth certificates, passports and any sentimental items. He was not sure about it at first, paused briefly and then he replied "Friday would be the best day for you both to enter the house without being seen." He explained that no one was going to be at the house for two hours before 1pm. I looked over at Tariq, who was seated beside me and asked him if Friday was fine with him to drive us to the house, he said yes and so I confirmed the secret meeting with Hamid.

Once I had ended my call with Hamid I took a few moments to think about what I was getting myself and Aisha into. I knew I was putting us in danger by entering the house, knowing full well that we had been threatened by Yasmin, Fatima and her violent husband but I just had to go back for one last time. As I continued to think about Friday it suddenly dawned on me that I had not discussed any of this with Aisha and I just assumed she would be going along with me. Aisha was in the kitchen cooking so I headed downstairs to tell her what I had arranged. Once I told her she stopped what she was doing and said it was far too dangerous, she went on to say "how can you be sure you trust Hamid? What if the rest of the family are aware that Hamid is speaking to us and they are setting up a trap for us!" I shook my head in disbelief, "I trust him." I said. "Anyway we only have a maximum of two hours to collect what we need and I doubt we will stay there very long." Aisha was not convinced but truth be told neither was I. I had doubts and there was something which did not feel right to me, I just could not pinpoint it and so I chose to push it to the back of my mind.

Friday arrived; the day for Aisha and I collect our belongings. We all set out early this particular morning to avoid any traffic as the last thing we wanted was to be late and miss our opportunity. I called Hamid just before we set off to make sure everything was still as arranged and if he was still sure no one else was going to be at the house. Hamid seemed sure there was not a problem and said he would see us shortly.

We arrived an hour later and Tariq parked a few streets away from the house near the shade of some red maples. We were early so I waited a few minutes before I called Hamid to tell him we had arrived. Hamid instructed us to walk up to the rear entrance of the house where he said he would be waiting. My stomach began to churn as I looked over at Aisha and said "It's time, come on lets go," Tariq asked me to keep my mobile phone on me at all times just in case. I was now starting to feel afraid; I felt sick, nervous as If we were going to get caught and if we did we would not be able to leave the house.

Aisha and I quickly left the car and walked the short distance to the house. As we walked up the narrow footpath which led to the small back garden, I noticed Hamid had already opened the gate for us and was patiently waiting at the back door. I gave Hamid a warm hug and asked him if he was well, he smiled and said yes. He nudged Aisha lovingly who then gave him a friendly nudge back she peeked through the door and whispered "Are you sure no one else is home?" Hamid assured us once more and said we did not have much time and he then said "Abdul will be home in an hour." "Oh my god!" I said in a panic. I took hold of Aisha's right arm and dragged her along with me as I entered the house without hesitation.

In the first moments of entering the house, my heart felt like it had stopped beating. I felt frozen, scared, trapped, like I was captured and in prison again. I had escaped but stepping foot inside and hearing the back door close behind me almost took my breath away. Hearing the door close felt so final, it felt like I had never escaped in the first place. Escaping was only a dream and now being in the house was a reality.

The house looked dark even though the sun was shining brightly through the bay window in the dining room. I felt a chill down my spine as I walked deeper inside the house. There was an eerie atmosphere which seemed to linger as we made our way through the kitchen, hallway and then to the ground floor landing. Aisha and I paused for a moment at the foot of the staircase which led to the second floor bedrooms. We looked at one another as if to say "This is it, there's no going back." I took a deep breath to help me as I geared myself up for entering our bedroom. Once we had walked up the unlucky thirteen steps of the staircase, I could not help but notice the clutter. There were black bin liners resting against the wall which were filled to the brim with our clothing. The bags were dumped outside Yasmin's bedroom as though she had the rights to our clothing now. I entered our bedroom first, closely followed by Aisha and then Hamid. What I walked into did not surprise me in the slightest. Our belongings lay scattered around the room, not a square foot of carpet was visible. It looked as though we had been burgled.

As I took a closer look inside the room I began search for the items I came to the house for, I noticed a number of my personal belongings were missing. I asked Hamid where they were and he suggested I take a look inside Yasmin's bedroom. I entered Yasmin's bedroom and there they were, my designer perfume, make-up and hair straightener. My belongings were laid out on her dressing table as if they were rightfully hers. As I took a closer look I noticed a few of my best pieces of jewellery, they too were now in her possession. Yasmin had helped herself to my belongings; it was as though she took first dibs on what she wanted. I chose not to take my items back as the last thing I wanted was for her to know that I had been inside the house without her knowing. Instead I walked away and concentrated on what I had really come for.

When I returned to our bedroom, Aisha was searching through her belongings; she too was disgusted with the way Yasmin and the others had trashed our room. A number of Aisha's belongings were also missing. Hamid told us that he tried to stop Yasmin from searching through our belonging but she refused to listen to him, in the end he felt like he could do nothing but stand back and not get involved as she already blamed him for us leaving.

As I gathered my belongings I kept a close eye on the time, it was nearly 12pm. I was getting anxious now and feared we would not leave the house before Abdul returned home. Tariq called to ask if everything was fine, I told him about what Yasmin had done to the bedroom, he advised me not to think too much about it and to only concentrate on what we came for and to leave the house as soon as we could.

As I carried on searching for my identification documents I was struggling to find my passport. I knew where I had kept it but it was not there, it had been taken. I asked Hamid if he had seen it and he replied no. I then went into Yasmin's bedroom again and searched her wardrobe and her chest of drawers, but the passport was nowhere to be seen. Then I searched under her mattress and found a number of letters addressed to Aisha and me. She had kept these hidden and all of them had been opened. The letters were clearly marked personal and should only have been opened by the addressee. One by one I opened each envelope which was addressed to me and to my horror I learnt that Yasmin had been withdrawing money from my newly opened back account. I had taken out a student loan before leaving the house but my cash card and pin number had only arrived at the house after I had left. I got a strange feeling at the pit of my stomach as I took in what I had just learnt. It had made me feel sick to my stomach.

I gathered up all of the letters addressed for me and Aisha. I didn't care at this moment in time if Yasmin came to realise, I had been inside the house and in her room. Once I had lifted the bulk of letters from under her mattress, I came across my passport and Aisha's too. I remembered from previously sharing a room with Yasmin that she would hide things under her mattress. I am pleased to have recovered my passport but I felt Yasmin must have known that I would return to the house for it otherwise why would she have hidden it?

I grabbed the passports and letters and headed back to our bomb-site of a bedroom. We had just about gathered what we came for when Hamid heard the front door open. He rushed to leave the room, he returned and said "Abdul, he is home!"

"What" we whispered in panic? "Oh my God, what do we do now?" I said as I looked at Aisha in fear. She was speechless, Hamid asked us both to keep quiet and to stay in the room until he got back. As Aisha and I waited we could hear Abdul ask him what he was going to have for his lunch and whether there was any leftover curry from the night before. "Nothing has changed then." I quietly whispered to Aisha. Abdul never really put much thought into what he consumed, leftover takeaway was normal for him.

Half an hour had gone by and Hamid still had not returned, we were getting worried. Aisha and I tried to find a spot to hide in amongst all the mess. We then settled on crouching on the floor beside my single bed which had been pushed against the window sill. It was a tight squeeze with just enough space for us to hide in, hopefully without being discovered.

As we hid with our hands on the floor, I took an opportunity to text Tariq, to tell him what was happening just in case he became worried as it was approaching 1pm. Within a minute or two I received a reply from him which read "Shit! Do you want me to do something?"

"Like what?" I replied back.

"Come and get you?" he replied.

"No you can't, it's too risky. Abdul will find us or see you in the house." To my relief, Tariq then replied and said he would wait for us in the car.

Aisha and I could hear a lot of movement coming from below the floorboards. The doors were being slammed as Abdul walked from one room to another. The television was on loud and I could hear Hamid say "Turn the volume down". Then came the footsteps, the sound was getting louder and louder as it headed our way. Aisha and I ducked deeper towards the floor with the height of the headboard from the bed protecting us from being discovered. The door then opened and Hamid whispered, "Aisha, Samina are you still in here? It's okay Abdul is downstairs." I crawled from behind the protection of the bed and said, "When is he leaving so we can go?" Hamid looked fed up and annoyed and bluntly said, "He is staying; he's in the living room." I nervously stood up and looked out of the window towards the direction where Tariq was parked. I actually felt helpless and trapped and knowing Tariq was parked only streets away drove me to tears. Aisha took control of the situation and told me to pull myself together. She was determined to get us out of the house without Abdul seeing us.

Aisha asked Hamid if she thought Abdul was likely to leave the living room any time soon. Hamid seemed confident as he said "I doubt he will, he is watching his favourite show on ARY Digital and he is eating a large plate of chicken karahi, he is too fat and lazy to move from of his favoured spot on the sofa." Aisha suggested a plan, it would be risky but it was worth it if we could get away sooner rather than being stuck in the bedroom for hours. The longer we left it the harder it would be for us to get out and Yasmin, Laila and Nadia would have returned home.

The plan was for Hamid to act as a shield for us and to lead us out of the house while we walked a few steps behind him. We couldn't afford to hesitate as time was slipping away.

Aisha and I gathered our belongings and left the room closely following Hamid as he made his way down the stairs. We were all now at the bottom of the stairs a few footsteps away from leaving. Aisha and I only had the kitchen and back door to go through. Passing the living room was the hardest part, it was dangerous. As we passed, we tip-toed to ensure we didn't make any sound which could have diverted Abdul's attention away from the television and his lunch. We had finally made it. The race against time was over. Abdul had not seen us and we were on our way to the car.

When I reached the car, I slumped into the back seat with Aisha and let out a sigh of relief. Tariq did not utter a word as our facial expressions and body language were doing all the talking. I eventually broke the silence, crying out "Thank God that is over."

40 I live in hope

DURING THE COURSE of a few months Hamid stopped calling. He had stopped all communication, even his social networking page had disappeared. I felt he disapproved of us leaving the family home and for wanting to live our own lives on our own terms.

During the time I spent speaking to him it had become obvious to me that he had been brainwashed by Fatima and Yasmin and their destructive ways. I felt upset as Hamid was a hope for me, I hoped he would stay in contact with us and then maybe one day the rest of the family may follow suit but this hope was now shattered. Aisha was the only family member I had left and she only had me.

Our family were holding us back from following our dreams and this had resulted in them disowning us. Years of headache and trouble had led to Aisha and I breaking free and escaping to freedom. Over the years I have become stronger mentally and emotionally; the battle is not yet over. I regularly think about my family even though I know I could never go back to them as that would mean giving up my freedom. Yasmin and Fatima's dysfunctional relationships may play a big part their own children's lives which I am certain will be passed on from one generation to the next. Breaking free from the toxic relationship I once had with them was the hardest thing I have ever had to do.

Aisha found the situation highly traumatic and chose to suffer in silence for many years. I would hear her cry at night, I could tell she was feeling pain and missed the family. She has now learned to be stronger and this has strengthened our bond.

Tariq and I grew apart. I blamed my family for our break-up. We were always arguing and I became jealous of him seeing his family whereas I could no longer see or speak to mine - I felt left out. I missed my family and consequently blamed Tariq for this, I felt if I had not met Tariq I would still have a family.

I was treated for depression and it has taken me many years to overcome the trauma I suffered in my early life, it had followed me for many years. I suffered from stress and anxiety at a young age, which then lead into my adult life. I am now learning to control my anxiety and stress but I do have bad days. For many years I felt guilty for leaving my family and escaping my inevitable forced marriage. I felt my parents wherever they are must think very badly of me. I have not yet come to terms with never seeing my family again and the thought of never seeing my nieces and nephews breaks my heart. I hope one day reconciliation will happen but until then Aisha and I have accepted the situation and we are slowly working on healing from the pain we are in.

Aisha and I now have control of our own destiny and it is up to us to fulfil it to the best of our ability as we have fought very hard and gained a second chance in life.

I doubt the pain of losing my family will ever heal; time will never stand still and neither will the pain of our loss. I have learnt to live with the injustices I have faced and it has just made me a better person now.

No child should ever be disowned. Living a life of happiness is going to be my motivation and history for me will never repeat itself and I now understand it will be a life-long journey.

• THE END •

About the Author

Samina Younis was born and raised in England. She is a budding model and actress and has her own cosmetics boutique. She is a first time writer and began writing this book as a therapy for herself to overcome her tragic past. She felt she had to tell her true story to inspire other women to break free from their family controlled lives.

She has a passion for helping other people who may be in the same situation as she once was and she would like to inspire other women to follow their heart.

On a typical day you may find her working out at her local gymnasium. She enjoys travelling, reading and going to the cinema. She loves Italian food, eating doughnuts, baking, cooking and belly laughter.

Other titles availible from

Oxford eBooks

City of Storms

When top foreign correspondent Sean Brian flies into Manila in the Philippines as part of his Asian news beat, a typhoon and a political revolution are uppermost in his thoughts.

But what also awaits will turn his already busy life into a roller coaster of romance, adventure, elation and despair.

At the centre of this transformation is an infant boy child, born, abandoned and plunged into street poverty in the grim underbelly of an Asian metropolis.

This is the catalyst for a story ranging from the corrupt, violent world of back street city sex clubs and drug addiction, to the clean air of the Sulu Sea and the South Pacific; from the calm safety of an island paradise to the violent guerilla world of the notorious Golden Triangle and the southern Philippines archipeligo.

As we follow the child, Bagyo, into fledgling manhood, we can only wonder at the ripples that spread from one individual to engulf so many others – and at the injustice that still corrodes life on the mean streets of the world.

This is I, Elizabeth... but who cares?

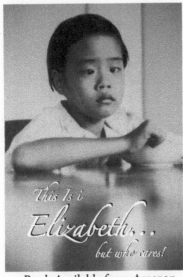

eBook Available from Amazon

When Elizabeth Poey discovered that she had cancer in 2008, her dream of writing a book about her life suddenly became an urgent item on her "To Do" list... and in 2010 when her cancer returned it occupied the number one slot on her "Bucket List".

In this book Elizabeth shares her experiences growing up in Singapore from the 1950's onwards. She records her teenage years and relationships with her extended family, dogs and above all her relationship with God.

Her beautifully recalled story is garnished with many colourful references to life in Singapore, the places, the language, the people... and of course the FOOD. Throughout the book, you will discover photographs of her life and the people closest to her.

As a highly spirited child, she was every teacher's nightmare until she grew up to become a teacher herself. Teacher training days were as fun as they were funny, and she recalls many wonderful episodes over her 36 year career in education.

The author humbly describes her book as "an autobiography of a nobody", but as you will read, her life has touched and inspired many from her beginnings in a simple Singaporean village to the heights of the Himalayas.

"This is I, Eliabeth.. but who cares - I know, God does."

The Dustman's Daughter

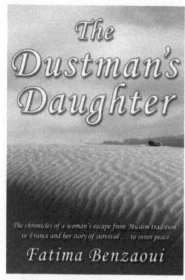

eBook available from Amazon

The Chronicles of a woman's escape from Muslim tradition in France and her story of survival … to inner peace.

This is the true story of Fatima Benzaoui, born to an Algerian immigrant family in Nanterre, France. She recounts her lifelong struggles against her strict Muslim family growing up in France to gain the education she so desperately wants to break free from the outdated and stifling traditions of her parents.

She finds both beauty and dogma of tradition in the deserts of the Sahara at her family home in Algeria where like many before her, she is faced with the spectre of forced marriage.

The girl, grows into a woman with a life-plan in her heart and the determination to make it come true, despite everything that mankind and nature throws at her.